P · O · O ·

RECORD
BREAKERS

QUEEN ALEXANDRA
BIRDWING, RAREST
BUTTERFLY

FIRST
HOUSEHOLD
MATCHES

SATURN,
PLANET WITH
MOST MOONS

OLDEST
FOOTBALL
BOOT

BUDWEISER ROCKET CAR,
FASTEST VEHICLE

P · O · C · K · E · T · S

RECORD BREAKERS

Written by

ANITA GANERI
AND CHRIS OXLADE

BERLINER'S RECORD PLAYER -
THE FIRST

PENGUINS,
FASTEST SWIMMING
BIRDS

WALRUS
SKULL,
LONGEST
TOOTH

DK

DORLING KINDERSLEY
London • New York • Moscow • Sydney

DK

A DORLING KINDERSLEY BOOK

Produced for Dorling Kindersley by
PAGE*One*, Cairn House, Elgiva Lane, Chesham,
Buckinghamshire HP5 2JD

Project directors	Bob Gordon, Helen Parker
Editor	Sarah Watson
Designer	Matthew Cook
DK team	Jane Yorke, Marcus James
Production	Joanne Rooke
Picture research	Caroline Allen, Christine Rista
Jacket design	Dean Price

Published in Great Britain by
Dorling Kindersley Limited, 9 Henrietta Street,
London WC2E 8PS

2 4 6 8 10 9 7 5 3 1

A CIP catalogue record for this book is available from
the British Library.

ISBN 0-7513-5661-1

Colour reproduction by Colourscan, Singapore
Printed and bound in Italy by L.E.G.O.

CONTENTS

ANGEL FALLS,
TALLEST IN
THE WORLD

LIONFISH,
ONE OF
THE MOST
POISONOUS FISH

COLUMBIA,
FIRST RE-USEABLE
SPACE SHUTTLE

WHEAT,
CHINA PRODUCES
THE MOST

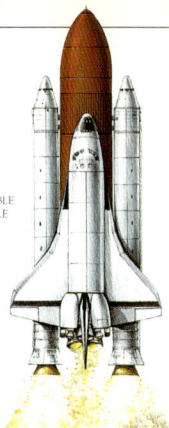

First balls,
Egypt 2000 bc

First
technicolor
film camera,
1920s

HOW TO USE THIS BOOK

THESE PAGES show you how to use *DK Pockets: Record Breakers*. The book is divided into six sections of photographs, comparative artworks, and record boxes. At the start of each section there is a picture page that illustrates a record, with a list of contents.

HEADING
This describes the subject of the page. This particular page is about sea mammals.

INTRODUCTION
This provides a clear overview of the subject. After reading this, you should have an idea what the pages are about.

CORNER CODING
The corners of the pages in each section are colour-coded as follows to remind you which section you are in.

- ■ PHYSICAL WORLD
- ■ LIVING WORLD
- ■ PEOPLE AND SOCIETY
- ■ SCIENCE AND TECHNOLOGY
- ■ ARTS AND THE MEDIA
- ■ SPORT

Heading

Corner coding

Introduction

Label

Annotation

Record tint box

LIVING WORLD

SEA MAMMALS

OF THE 4,000 mammal species, about 120 live in the sea. They include cetaceans (porpoises, whales, and dolphins), pinnipeds (seals and walruses), and sirenians (manatees and dugongs).

LARGEST MOUTH
The gigantic blue whale has the largest mouth of all animals. These tall jaw bones come from one of the last blue whales ever caught and are erected in the seaside town of Whitby, UK.

Blue whale

Blue whales are at the scales at 120 tonnes (118 tons)

WHALE AND DOLPHIN RECORDS

Largest	Loudest	Thickest blubber
The blue whale is the largest animal alive today, measuring at least 33.5 m (110 ft) long. On land it would be squashed by its weight.	Blue whales are also the loudest sea mammals. Their "songs" register 188 decibels and can be heard 850 km (528 miles) away.	When feeding, a right whale's blubber, or fat beneath the skin, can be 60 cm (2 ft) thick. It protects the whale from the cold.
Fastest	**Longest song**	**Longest lived**
Killer whales are the speediest sea mammals, swimming at up to 55 km/h (34 mph).	The humpback whale's "song" lasts for half an hour and contains many different tones.	It is thought that fin whales reach a grand old age of 90–100 years.

LABELS
For extra clarity, some pictures have labels. They may give extra information, or identify a picture when it is not obvious from the text what it is.

CAPTIONS
Those illustrations that sit outside record boxes have an explanatory caption. This is because the record is unusual, or particularly noteworthy.

RUNNING HEADS

These remind you which section you are in. The top of the left-hand page gives the section name. The top of the right-hand page gives the subject.

RECORD BOXES

Most pages have record boxes, some with a coloured tint. Each record box is filled with specific information about records with a similar subject matter.

Running head

Record entry

Record box head

OLYMPIC WORLD RECORDS

FOR TODAY'S TOP athletes, winning an Olympic gold medal is a dream come true, the pinnacle of their athletic careers. For others, simply taking

SEA MAMMALS

PINNIPED RECORDS

Largest
The southern elephant seal is enormous. Males can grow up to 6.5 m (21 ft) long and weigh 3,500 kg (3½ tons).

Fastest
For short journeys, Californian sea lions can swim through the water at speeds of up to 40 km/h (25 mph).

Longest whiskers
A male Antarctic fur seal was found to have whiskers that have grown into a huge, spiralling tusk that can be as long as 1 m (3¼ ft).

Heaviest
It is estimated that there may be as few as 500 wild Mediterranean monk seals left.

Longest journey
From their winter breeding grounds in Mexico to their summer feeding grounds in the Bering Sea, grey whales travel up to 20,000 km (12,500 miles) a year

Smallest blow
The blue whale's blow reaches 12 m (39 ft), as high as six tall people.

Fastest

Longest teeth
The narwhal, has only two teeth. In males, one tooth grows into a huge, spiralling tusk that can be as long as 3 m (10 ft).

Unlike other whales, the blue whale raises its tail when it dives

20 divers could swim head-to-tail alongside a Blue whale

Bottlenose dolphin

Dolphins sound

Deepest diver
Sperm whales can dive to depths of more than 2,000 m (6,561 ft).

MOST FAMOUS DOLPHIN
Historically, dolphins and people have had a special relationship. In the well-known TV show *Flipper*, a bottlenose dolphin and a young boy become friends.

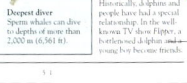

Caption

ATHLETE RECORDS

First black African gold medallist
In 1960, Abebe Bikila ran the marathon barefoot and became the first black African to win gold.

First brothers to win Olympic medal
Lottie and Reggie Doherty won the men's tennis doubles at the 1900 Olympics held in Paris, France.

First perfect ten
At the 1976 Montreal Games, Romanian gymnast Nadia Comaneci scored the first ever perfect ten.

Oldest female Olympic gold medallist
Lis Marielos of Romania was 36 years old when she won the discus at the 1968 Olympics in Mexico.

Greatest record-breaker
In the 1968 Mexico Olympics, American Bob Beamon increased the long jump record by 55 cm (21½ in)

FASTEST OLYMPIC RUNNER
Jesse Owens, USA, defied the Nazi idea of white supremacy at the 1936 Berlin Olympics and won four gold medals.

OLYMPIC JUMPING EVENTS

EVENT	ATHLETE	DISTANCE
High jump	(m) C. Austin	2.39 m
	(f) S. Kostadinova	2.09 m
Long jump	(m) B. Beamon	8.90 m
	(f) J. Joyner-Kersee	7.40 m
Triple jump	(m) J. Edwards	18.29 m
	(f) I. Kravets	15.33 m
Pole vault	(m) S. Gulfrone	5.92 m

OLYMPIC THROWING RECORDS

EVENT	WEIGHT	ATHLETE	DISTANCE
Javelin	(m) 2 kg	J. Zelezny	89.66 m
	(f) 0.6 kg	P. Felke	74.68 m
Discus	(m) 2 kg	L. Riedel	69.40 m
	(f) 1 kg	M. Hellmann	83.22 m
Shot put	(m) 7.26 kg	U. Timmermann	22.47 m
	(f) 4 kg	I. Slupianek	22.41 m
Hammer	(m) 7.26 kg	S. Litvinov	84.80 m

Olympic record table

RECORD TABLE

Clear, concise record tables group statistics together, for example an athlete's name, event, distance, and time.

ANNOTATION

Picked out in *italics*, annotation points out noteworthy features of an illustration or photograph. It is usually accompanied by a leader line and can give extra information.

INDEX

At the back of the book you will find a comprehensive index that alphabetically lists subjects and records included in the book.

Physical World

Longest mountain chain: Andes, South America

THE UNIVERSE

BORN FROM A massive explosion called the "Big Bang", about 15 billion years ago, the universe consists of the Sun, moon, stars, planets, and 100 billion galaxies.

STAR RECORDS

Nearest star to Earth
Our closest star is Proxima Centauri, 4.2 light years away.

Brightest star
Seen from Earth, Sirius A shines 24 times more brightly than the Sun.

Most luminous star
Eta Carinae gives off 6,500,000 times more light than the Sun.

Smallest star
White dwarf star LP 327-16 is just 1,700 km (1,056 miles) wide.

Faintest star
RG 0058.8-2807 is a million times less bright than the Sun.

Oldest star
Some stars high above the Milky Way are 14 billion years old.

Largest star
Betelgeuse is 500 times wider than the Sun.

Brightest supernova
The SN 1006 supernova (exploding star) was first seen in AD 1006. It glowed for two years.

Oldest star map
A painted star map from 25 BC was found in 1987 on a Chinese tomb.

CONSTELLATION RECORDS

Largest constellation
Of 88 constellations, the largest, Hydra (the Watersnake), covers six per cent of the sky.

Smallest constellation
The tiny Crux Australis, or Southern Cross, contains only five stars.

Largest zodiacal constellation
Virgo is the largest of the 12 zodiacal constellations.

Smallest zodiacal constellation
The stars of Capricorn have the smallest area.

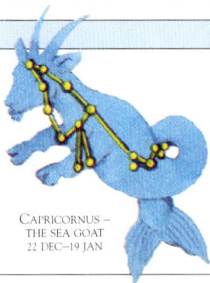

CAPRICORNUS –
THE SEA GOAT
22 DEC–19 JAN

GALAXY RECORDS

First galaxy
The first galaxies were formed about 14 billion years ago, about one billion years after the "Big Bang" explosion.

Furthest galaxy visible to the naked eye
The Andromeda Galaxy is 2,200,000 light years away from the Earth.

Largest galaxy
Lying in the Abell 2029 cluster, some 1070 million light years away, the largest galaxy is 5.5 million light years wide.

Brightest galaxy
The IRAS F10214 + 4724 galaxy is 300 million million times as bright as the the Sun.

Most distant object
Quasar PC 1247 + 3406, an exploding centre of a distant galaxy, is 13.2 billion light years away.

Closest galaxy
The Sagittarius Dwarf galaxy is the nearest to Earth outside our own galaxy, the Milky Way.

LONGEST TAIL
Many meteorites, comets, and asteroids float between the planets of our Solar System. Comets, chunks of debris and ice, have glowing tails. The longest – 330 million km (205 million miles) – belonged to the Great Comet of 1843.

COMET, METEOR, AND ASTEROID RECORDS

Most frequently seen
The comet Encke returns every 3.3 years.

Earliest comet
Appearances of Halley's Comet can be traced back to about 240 BC.

Closest to Earth
The nearest a comet has come to Earth is about 1,200,000 km (750,000 miles), when Lexell's Comet whizzed past in July 1770.

Largest meteorite
A meteorite crashed to Earth in Namibia, southern Africa, and weighed as much as eight elephants.

Oldest meteorite
Carbonaceous chondrites are 4.55 billion years old.

Largest asteroid
Ceres, first seen in 1801, measures 930 km (578 miles) across.

Brightest asteroid
Vesta has a reflective surface and is the only asteroid that you can see without a telescope.

VESTA

Solar system: planets and moons

The part of the Universe that we live in is called the Solar System. It is made up of nine planets, including Earth, that orbit the Sun with their moons, asteroids, comets, and meteorites.

PLUTO

PLANET RECORDS

Jupiter has a stormy atmosphere

Largest planet
Measuring 143,000 km (88,860 miles) around its equator, Jupiter is bigger than all the other planets put together.

Smallest, coldest, and furthest from Sun
Pluto is just 2,284 km (1,419 miles) wide and has a chilling surface temperature of -230°C (-382°F). It is also the outermost planet, at 5,914 million km (3,675 million miles) from the Sun.

Hottest planet
Venus has a scorching hot surface temperature of 465°C (869°F), and is the brightest planet.

Only planet with life
Earth is the only planet known to have the right amount of oxygen and water to support life.

Closest to the Sun
Mercury lies only 58 million km (36 million miles) away from the Sun. It is one of the inner planets, with Venus, Mars, and Earth.

Fastest orbiting planet
A Mercury year lasts 88 days, the time it takes to orbit the Sun. The planet orbits at 170,000 km/h (105,000 mph).

Slowest planet
As it is so far away from the Sun, Pluto takes 248.5 Earth years to orbit the Sun.

Closest planet to Earth
Venus is the nearest planet to our own, lying about 42 million km (26 million miles) away. Its distance from the Sun is 108 million km (67 million miles).

JUPITER

MOON RECORDS

Largest Moon crater
Bailly crater, near the Moon's South Pole, measures a vast 295 km (183 miles) across.

Highest Moon mountain
The tallest mountain on the Moon rises 7,830 m (25,688 ft), about 1 km (½ mile) lower than Earth's highest point, Mount Everest.

Largest moon
Ganymede, one of Jupiter's moons, weighs twice as much as Earth's Moon.

Planet with most moons
Saturn has 18 moons. Titan, the largest, is 5,150 km (3,200 miles) in width.

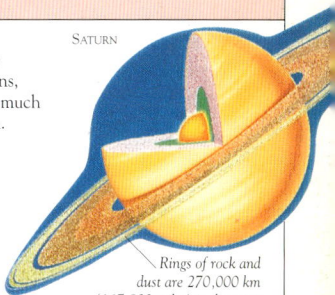

SATURN

Rings of rock and dust are 270,000 km (167,800 miles) in diameter

SUN RECORDS

Closest star
Lying a distance of about 150 million km (93 million miles) from Earth, the Sun is our closest and most important star. Without its heat and light, there would be no life.

Longest solar eclipse
In June 1955, an eclipse of the Sun lasted for seven minutes and eight seconds.

Hottest spot on Sun
The Sun's core reaches a melting 14 million°C (57 million°F).

Largest sunspot
Sunspots are dark patches that occur when the Sun's heat flow is blocked by its magnetic field. The biggest was 35 times Earth's area.

Largest solar flare
In 1946, a plume of flaming hydrogen gas, arched 700,000 km (435,000 miles) from the Sun in one hour.

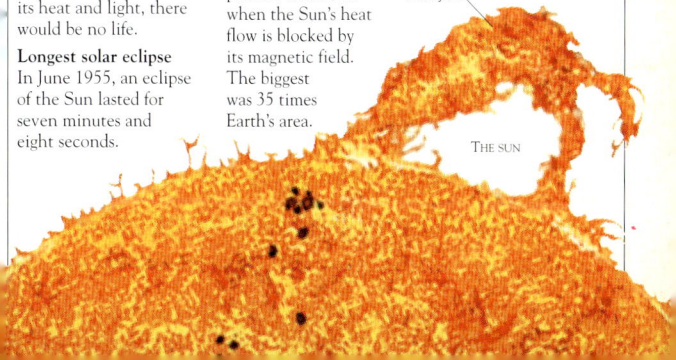

Solar flare

THE SUN

OCEANS AND SEAS

SEA WATER COVERS more than two-thirds of the Earth. It lies within five oceans – the Pacific, Atlantic, Indian, Southern, and Arctic. Together, the oceans contain 97 per cent of all the world's water.

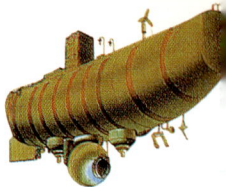

DEEPEST DIVE
In 1960, the bathyscaphe *Trieste*, dived 10,911 m (35,800 ft) into the Pacific Marianas Trench.

OCEAN AND SEA RECORDS

Largest ocean
The Pacific covers a third of the Earth, at 166,241,000 sq km (64,186,000 sq miles).

Smallest ocean
At 12 times smaller than the Pacific, the Arctic is 13,223,700 sq km (5,106,000 sq miles).

Deepest ocean
The Pacific has an average depth of 4,200 m (13,800 ft).

Shallowest ocean
The Arctic is 1,300 m (4,300 ft) deep on average. It is frozen solid for most of the year.

Saltiest water
Average ocean salinity is 3.5 per cent. That of the Red Sea is 4.2 per cent.

Biggest sea
The South China Sea covers 2,974,600 sq km (1,148,493 sq miles).

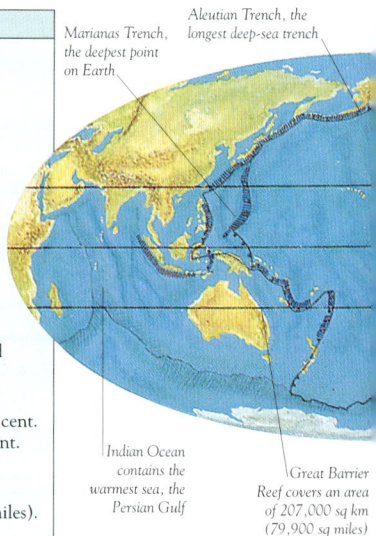

Marianas Trench, the deepest point on Earth

Aleutian Trench, the longest deep-sea trench

Indian Ocean contains the warmest sea, the Persian Gulf

Great Barrier Reef covers an area of 207,000 sq km (79,900 sq miles)

OCEAN FEATURE RECORDS

Deepest sea trench
The Marianas Trench, in the Pacific, is the deepest point on Earth, plunging 10,924 m (35,840 ft) into the sea.

Highest seamount
The tallest underwater mountain, Great Meteor Tablemount in the Atlantic, is 8,700 m (28,500 ft), as high as Mount Everest.

Longest ocean mountain range
The Mid-Atlantic Ridge runs for 11,265 km (7,000 miles) down the middle of the Atlantic.

Longest coastline
Canada's vast coastline measures 90,908 km (56,490 miles).

Largest bay
The vast shoreline of Hudson Bay in Canada, continues for 12,268 km (7,623 miles).

Tallest wave
In February 1933, *USS Ramapo* recorded a wave 34 m (112 ft) tall.

Greatest ocean current
Also known as the West Wind Drift, the Antarctic Circumpolar Current flows at a rate of 130 million cu m (4.3 billion cu ft) per second.

Highest tides
Tides in the Bay of Fundy, Canada, can rise more than 15 m (49 ft).

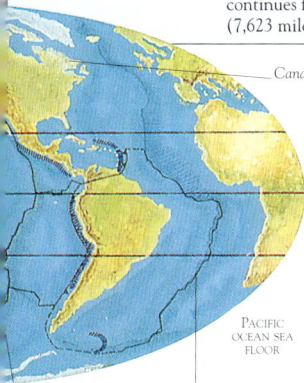

Canada has the world's longest coastline

PACIFIC OCEAN SEA FLOOR

Pacific Ocean is the largest, widest, and deepest ocean

Mid-Atlantic Ridge is the longest mountain chain in the world

LARGEST CORAL REEF
The Great Barrier Reef stretches for 2,028 km (1,260 miles) along the coast of Queensland in northeastern Australia. It covers twice the area of Iceland.

THE WORLD'S FRESHWATER

ONLY THREE PER CENT of the Earth's water is fresh. Most is frozen in glaciers and ice sheets. Less than one per cent is contained in the world's lakes and rivers, and underground.

Angel Falls, Venezuela

Utigård, Norway

Yosemite, USA

Sutherland, New Zealand

HIGHEST WATERFALL
Crashing down from the great height of 979 m (3,212 ft), Angel Falls in Venezuela is the world's tallest waterfall. Its greatest single drop is an amazing 807 m (2,648 ft).

Eiffel Tower, France

Victoria Falls, Zambia/Zimbabwe

Niagara Falls, USA/Canada

RIVER RECORDS

Longest river
The River Nile in Egypt flows for 6,695 km (4,160 miles) from its source to its delta.

Biggest river
The River Amazon is shorter than the Nile but holds more water. Each minute, 95,000 litres (20,900 gallons) flow out into the sea.

Shortest river
Flowing to the Pacific Ocean, the D River in Oregon, USA, is just 37 m (121 ft) long.

Largest delta
The delta of the Ganges and Brahmaputra rivers in India and Bangladesh covers about 75,000 sq km (29,000 sq miles).

Largest river basin
Drained by the mighty Amazon, the largest basin covers more than seven million sq km (three million sq miles) in South America.

LAKE RECORDS

Largest lake
Covering 371,800 sq km (143,500 sq miles), the Caspian Sea in Russia and Iran is called a sea because its water is salty.

Deepest lake
Lake Baikal in Siberia, Russia, is 1,620 m (5,315 ft) at its deepest point. It is also the world's largest lake if compared by volume.

Largest freshwater lake
Lake Superior, one of the USA's Great Lakes, covers 82,350 sq km (31,800 sq miles).

Lake Baikal: 22,995 cubic km (5,519 cubic miles)

Highest lake
Lake Titicaca lies 3,810 m (12,500 ft) up in the Andes Mountains of Peru and Bolivia.

Lake Superior: 12,174 cubic km (2,921 cubic miles)

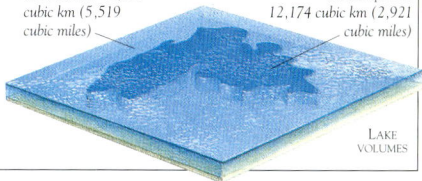

LAKE VOLUMES

GLACIER RECORDS

Fastest moving glacier
Most glaciers creep down mountains at 2.5–60 cm (1–24 in) per day, but Greenland's Quarayaq glacier flows at 20 m (66 ft) per day.

Longest glacier
The Lambert-Fisher Ice Passage in Antarctica is approximately 515 km (320 miles) long.

Thickest icesheet
Records show that the ice that covers Wilkes Land in Antarctica is an incredible 5 km (3 miles) thick in some places.

Largest iceberg
The biggest recorded iceberg covered an area the size of Belgium. It was more than 335 km (208 miles) long and 97 km (60 miles) wide.

Tallest iceberg
An iceberg with a grand height of 167 m (548 ft) was seen in 1958, in Greenland.

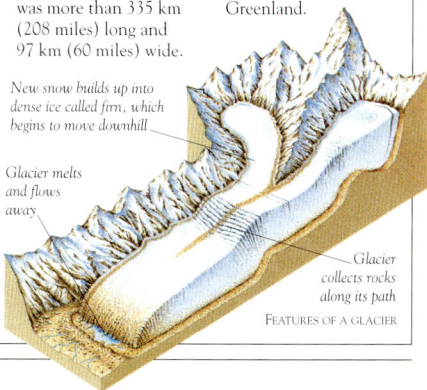

New snow builds up into dense ice called firn, which begins to move downhill

Glacier melts and flows away

Glacier collects rocks along its path

FEATURES OF A GLACIER

MOUNTAINS, VALLEYS, AND CAVES

OVER MILLIONS of years, the Earth's moving tectonic plates have forced the crust to buckle and fold. High mountain peaks and deep valleys have been formed, carved into shape by the attacking forces of the wind and rain, and by glaciers.

LARGEST PLATEAU
Covering 1,850,000 sq km (714,285 sq miles), the high Tibetan plateau lies in Asia.

HIGH POINTS

Highest mountain
Mount Everest, on the Tibet/Nepal border, rises 8,848 m (29,028 ft) above sea level.

Highest range
All 35 of the world's highest mountains are found in the Himalaya-Karakoram range, Asia.

Longest range
The volcanic peaks and mountains of the Andes stretch for 7,200 km (4,474 miles) down the western side of South America, passing through Colombia, Ecuador, Peru, Chile, Bolivia, and Argentina.

Highest unclimbed peak
Kankar Punsum stands 7,541 m (24,741 ft) tall on the border between Tibet and Bhutan.

Tallest sea mountain
Mauna Kea rises 10,205 m (33,480 ft) from the sea floor to form a Hawaiian island.

Everest, 8,848 m (29,028 ft)
HIGHEST MOUNTAINS
K2, 8,611 m (28,250 ft)
Kanchenjunga, 8,597 m (28,208 ft)
Lhotse I, 8,511 m (27,923 ft)
Makalu I, 8,481 m (27,824 ft)

LOW POINTS

Deepest valley
The Yarlung Zangbo valley is more than 5,000 m (16,404 ft) deep. It runs through the Himalayas in Tibet.

Lowest point on Earth
The shore of the Dead Sea lies 400 m (1,312 ft) below sea level, but the lake itself plunges down 728 m (2,388 ft).

Largest depression
The Caspian Sea basin in Russia and Iran covers more than 518,000 sq km (200,000 sq miles). Two-thirds is lake.

LARGEST GORGE
The USA's spectacular Grand Canyon, in Arizona, is more than 1.5 km (1 mile) deep.

US CAVES AND CANYONS
Here, the Mammoth Cave system, the world's longest, is compared to the canyons of Arizona.

King's Canyon, 49 km (30 miles)

Hell's Canyon, 201 km (125 miles)

Grand Canyon, 446 km (277 miles)

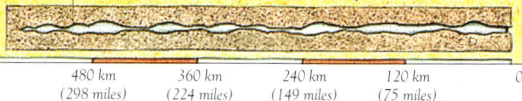

Mammoth Cave system, 567 km (352 miles)

480 km (298 miles)	360 km (224 miles)	240 km (149 miles)	120 km (75 miles)	0

CAVE RECORDS

Largest cave chamber
Malaysia's Sarawak Chamber is 700 m (2,296 ft) long.

Largest water cave
Mexico's Nohoch Na Chich caves continue for 24,000 m (7,873 ft).

Tallest stalagmite
An ancient stalagmite in the Czech Republic is 32 m (105 ft) tall.

Longest stalactite
A stalactite growing in an Irish cave is 6.2 m (20½ ft) long.

STALAGMITE IN KRÁSNOHORSKA CAVE, CZECH REPUBLIC

The tallest stalagmite is as high as 16 people

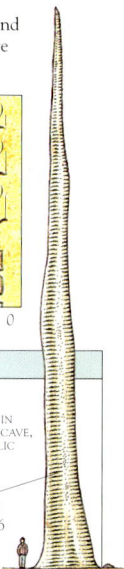

CLIMATE AND WEATHER

THE LONG-TERM pattern of temperature and conditions in an area is its climate. Weather is the daily state of the atmosphere, affected by the Sun, wind, and water vapour.

CONTINENTAL EXTREMES
This diagram shows both the hottest and coldest temperatures for each of the seven continents.

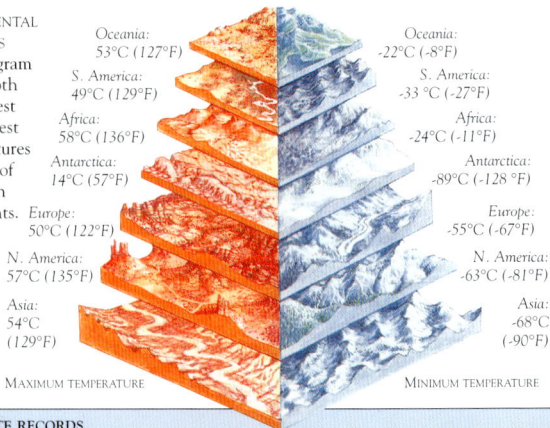

Oceania: 53°C (127°F)
S. America: 49°C (129°F)
Africa: 58°C (136°F)
Antarctica: 14°C (57°F)
Europe: 50°C (122°F)
N. America: 57°C (135°F)
Asia: 54°C (129°F)

Oceania: -22°C (-8°F)
S. America: -33°C (-27°F)
Africa: -24°C (-11°F)
Antarctica: -89°C (-128°F)
Europe: -55°C (-67°F)
N. America: -63°C (-81°F)
Asia: -68°C (-90°F)

MAXIMUM TEMPERATURE

MINIMUM TEMPERATURE

CLIMATE RECORDS

Hottest place (average)
Dallol, Ethiopia, has a temperature of 34.4°C (94°F) in the shade.

Coldest place (average)
Polus Nedostupnost (Pole of Inaccessibility) is usually -58°C (-72°F).

Highest temperature
A sizzling high of 58°C (136°F) was recorded at Azizia, Libya, in 1922.

Lowest temperature
In 1983, at Vostok, Antarctica, -89°C (-192°F), was recorded.

Sunniest place
The Eastern Sahara has sunshine for 90 per cent of its daylight hours.

Driest place
Chile's Atacama Desert has, on average, 0.5 mm (½ in) of rain per year.

WEATHER RECORDS

Fastest wind
In 1934, a 371-km/h (231-mph) gust of wind was recorded at Mt Washington, USA.

World's windiest place
In Commonwealth Bay, Antarctica, gales howl at 320 km/h (199 mph).

Highest pressure
Pressure of 1083.8 mb brought clear skies to Siberia, Russia, in 1968.

Lowest pressure
Pressure dipping to 870 mb causes cyclones at Typhoon Tip in the South Pacific.

Highest clouds
Wispy cirrus clouds drift 13,700 m (44,947 ft) high – 5,000 m (16,400 ft) above Mt Everest.

Lowest clouds
Stratus clouds form at 460 m (1509 ft), as low as some skyscrapers.

RAIN AND SNOW RECORDS

Greatest rainfall
In March 1952, the island of Réunion in the Indian Ocean received 18.7 cm (74 in) of rain in just 24 hours.

Largest raindrops
Raindrops are usually 1.5 mm (¹⁄₁₆ in) wide, but can be as big as peas.

Most rainy days
Mt Wai-'ale-'ale, in Hawaii, receives rain for about 350 days of each year.

Greatest snowfall
Annually, enough snow falls at Mt Rainier, USA, to cover a third of the Statue of Liberty.

HEAVIEST HAILSTONES
Hailstones as heavy as tenpin bowling balls fell in Kansas, USA, during September 1970.

MOST LIGHTNING STRIKES
American park ranger Roy Sullivan was struck by lightning seven times in 35 years, and survived!

THUNDER AND LIGHTNING RECORDS

Highest thunderclouds
Black cumulonimbus clouds hover at 16 km (10 miles) high.

Most thundery days
In Java, Indonesia, and around Lake Victoria, Africa, it thunders on 200–250 days a year.

Fastest lightning flash
When returning from the ground to a cloud, lightning can travel at 140,000 km/h (87,000 mph).

Longest lightning flash
Lightning flashes can be 32 km (20 miles) long.

NATURAL PHENOMENA

FROM EARTHQUAKES and volcanoes, to hurricanes and floods, the Earth's natural phenomena are forces to be reckoned with. At best, they pass unnoticed; at worst, they leave a trail of devastation.

VOLCANO RECORDS

Red-hot molten lava

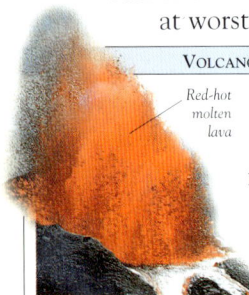

Largest active volcano
The dome of Mauna Loa, Hawaii, is 4,170 m (13,681 ft) high and 100 km (62 miles) wide.

Longest lava flow
In 1783, an eruption of Laki, in southeast Iceland, caused a lava flow that stretched 70 km (43½ miles).

Greatest eruption
About 92,000 people died when Tambora, in Indonesia, threw up enough ash to lower it by 1,250 m (4,101 ft).

Greatest explosion
In 1883, the eruption of Krakatoa, Indonesia, hurled rocks 55 km (34 miles) into the sky.

MAUNA LOA ERUPTING

EARTHQUAKE RECORDS

Worst damage
In 1923, an earthquake hit Japan, triggering fires that killed 144,000 people and destroyed some 575,000 homes.

Most deaths caused by an earthquake
A terrible earthquake in Shaanxi, China, in 1556, resulted in a death toll of 830,000 people.

Strongest known
In 1906, an earthquake in Colombia measured 8.9 on the Richter scale.

Longest lasting
A four-minute-long earthquake was recorded on 27 March 1964, in Alaska, USA.

EARTHQUAKE IN LOS ANGELES, 1994

TORNADO AND HURRICANE RECORDS

Strongest tornado
In 1931, a tornado in Minnesota, USA, lifted up an 83-tonne (82-ton) train.

Base of tornado can be 1 km (½ mile) wide

Rising air whips up into a destructive whirl

Tornadoes can move as fast as 55 km/h (35 mph)

TORNADO STRIKES

Most destructive tornado
In April 1989, Shaturia, Bangladesh, was hit by a violent tornado that left 1,300 people dead.

First named hurricane
Hurricanes were first given names in the 19th century by an Australian meteorologist called Clement "Wet" Wragge!

Most devastating hurricane
A hurricane that hit Bangladesh's Ganges Delta in November 1970 killed at least one million people.

TSUNAMI AND FLOOD RECORDS

Highest tsunami
Tsunamis are gigantic waves, triggered by earthquakes. The tallest on record appeared near Japan on 24 April 1971, rearing 85 m (279 ft) high, almost as tall as the Statue of Liberty.

Fastest tsunami
Tsunamis race across the sea at about 700 km/h (435 mph). The speediest have been recorded at 900 km/h (560 mph), as fast as a jet plane.

Worst flood
When the Huang He River in China flooded in October 1887, its waters drowned some 900,000 people.

It took the tsunami just 24 hours to travel between Chile and Japan

1971 TSUNAMI
RIPPLED ACROSS PACIFIC

MORE PHENOMENA

Greatest avalanche
The largest snowslide, 3,500,000 cubic m (120 million cu ft) of snow and ice, fell in the Italian Alps in 1885.

Worst landslide
In 1920, a landslide that was triggered by an earthquake in Gansu, China, killed 180,000 people.

Worst geyser disaster
Four people were killed when the world's tallest geyser – Waimangu in New Zealand – erupted.

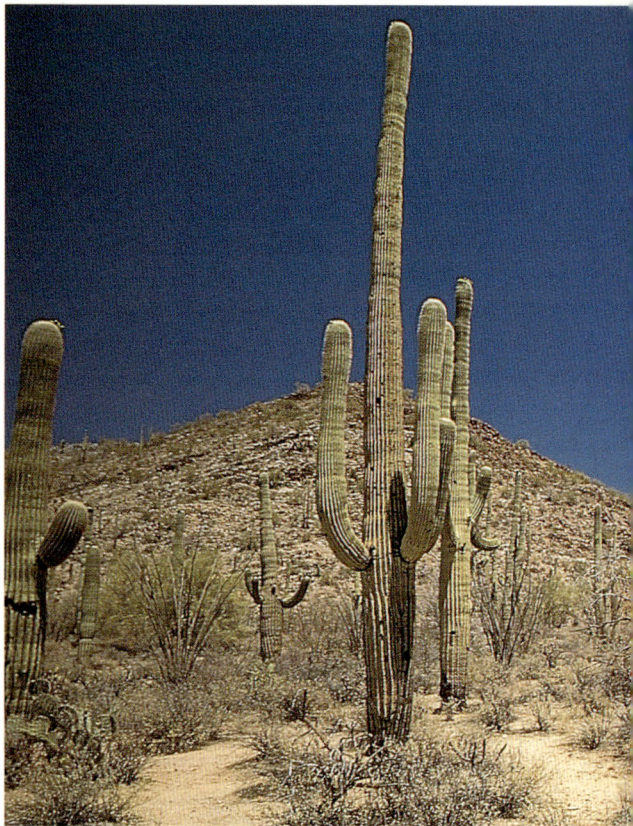

LIVING WORLD

Largest cactus: Saguaro, USA

DINOSAURS

ABOUT 225 MILLION years ago, a
group of scaly-skinned dinosaurs
ruled the Earth. They ranged
from the largest land animals
to have lived to creatures
no bigger than chickens.

OLDEST EGG
Discovered in the Gobi
Desert in the 1920s,
this *Protoceratops* egg was
one of the first complete
eggs found.

BAROSAURUS

LARGEST DINOSAURS
Sauropods, long-necked plant eaters,
were the largest dinosaurs. They
included the giant *Barosaurus*,
which grew to 24 m (79 ft) long and
weighed as much as eight elephants.

*PROTOCERATOPS
EGG*

SAUROPOD RECORDS

Biggest sauropod
Standing at up to 12 m
(39 ft) tall, the mighty
Brachiosaurus measured
22 m (72 ft) long.

Heaviest sauropod
With a weight of
80 tonnes (79 tons),
Antarctosaurus was
the heaviest sauropod.

Longest sauropod
The distance between
Breviparopus' footprints
suggests it was 48 m
(157 ft) long.

Longest neck
The amazing 10-m
(33-ft) long neck of
Mamenchisaurus is the
longest ever known.

HERBIVORE RECORDS

Largest footprint
Footprints made by a duck-billed dinosaur were 1.3 m (4¼ ft) long and 80 cm (31 in) wide.

Noisiest herbivore
Parasaurolophus had a tubular crest on its head, used to make deafening trumpeting sounds.

Long tail helped to balance the weight of such a long neck

Longest skeleton
The longest complete skeleton found is that of *Diplodocus*, a long-necked sauropod that grew to an incredible 26 m (85½ ft) long.

More than 50 people could stand side by side next to Diplodocus

Smallest brain
For its great size, *Stegosaurus* only had a tiny brain, smaller than a walnut.

Best defence
Ankylosaurus had a hard, bony club at the end of its tail for swinging at an enemy.

Diplodocus used its long neck to feed on leaves

DIPLODOCUS

CARNIVORE RECORDS

First found fossil
Originally thought to come from a giant man, the first fossil bone was discovered in 1677. It belonged to the mighty *Megalosaurus*.

Fastest carnivore
Coelurosaurs could speed along at about 40 km/h (25 mph) to catch prey.

Largest egg
Hypselosaurus laid giant eggs that were about the same volume as 60 chicken's eggs.

Largest brain
Small, speedy hunters, such as *Troodon*, had the largest brain in proportion to their size, but were not necessarily the most intelligent.

Smallest carnivore
The chicken-sized *Compsognathus* was so small it was less than 70 cm (28 in) long.

Largest claws
Therizinosaurus had the largest claws known, at 90 cm (35 in) long.

Largest teeth
The fearsome hunter *Tyrannosaurus rex* had sharp, dagger-like teeth that measured up to 18 cm (7 in) long and had serrated edges.

This human incisor is tiny compared to the dinosaur's tooth

HUMAN INCISOR

TYRANNOSAURUS REX TOOTH

Dinosaurs and reptiles

Sharing the world with some of Earth's
most ferocious creatures were other
prehistoric reptiles, both in the sea
and sky. They died out with the
dinosaurs, 65 million years ago.

*Crocodile-like jaws
were lined with
sharp teeth*

LARGEST PREDATOR
Tyrannosaurus rex was the largest of
the carnosaurs, or flesh-eaters, and one
of the fiercest creatures in the theropod
group. It stood 12 m (39 ft) tall, weighing
some 7.5 tonnes (7.4 tons).

EARLIEST DINOSAUR
The Argentinian carnivorous
Eoraptor lived 228 million years
ago. It walked on two legs, and
was about the size of a dog.

THEROPOD RECORDS

First theropod
Coelophysis lived in North
America during the Triassic
period, 220 million years ago.

First to be named
In 1824, an English professor
named his finding of bones
Megalosaurus, or "big lizard".

Most intelligent
Large-brained *Dromaeosaurids*
were the cleverest dinosaurs.

Last living theropod
Tyrannosaurus rex roamed
the Earth as recently as
65 million years ago.

TYRANNOSAURUS
REX

*Powerful
legs hold
down prey*

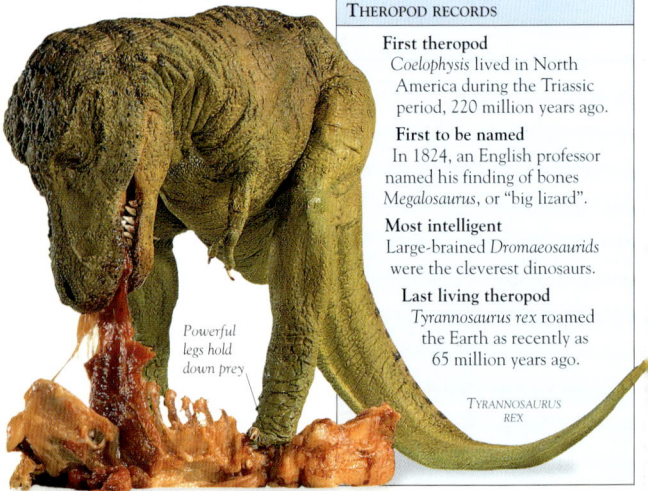

First flying vertebrate
Pterosaurs flew around conifer forests 245 million years ago.

Most famous flyer
Perhaps the most famous prehistoric flyer, *Pterodactylus* was only the size of a sparrow. It probably fed on insects.

Boniest head
Pteranodon had a 6-m (20-ft) wingspan and a 1-m (3-ft) long bony crest on its head to balance its heavy beak.

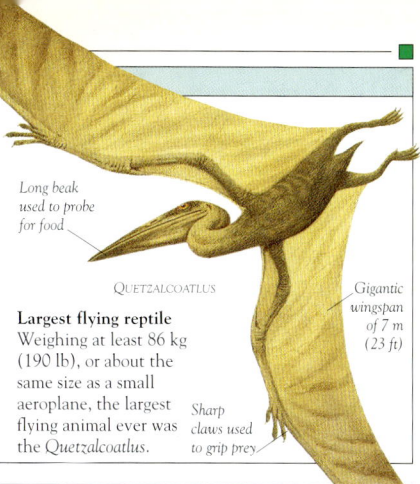

Long beak used to probe for food

QUETZALCOATLUS

Gigantic wingspan of 7 m (23 ft)

Largest flying reptile
Weighing at least 86 kg (190 lb), or about the same size as a small aeroplane, the largest flying animal ever was the *Quetzalcoatlus*.

Sharp claws used to grip prey

OCEAN REPTILE RECORDS

Biggest ocean reptile
With a 15 m (49 ft) body and a head of 3 m (10 ft), the giant *Kronosaurus* swam in the seas around Australia about 80 million years ago.

Biggest sea turtle
Archelon was a massive sea turtle that lived about 85 million years ago. It weighed at least 4 tonnes (3.9 tons) and was the size of a truck.

Most ferocious
Kronosaurus and *Pliosaurus* were two of the most vicious sea reptiles. Both had about 80 sharp, spiky teeth, each measuring over 20 cm (8 in) in length.

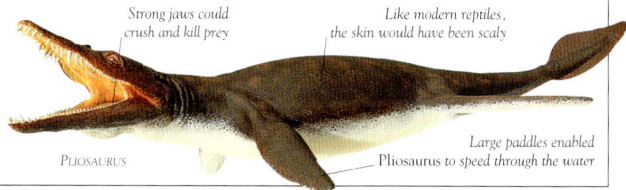

Strong jaws could crush and kill prey

Like modern reptiles, the skin would have been scaly

PLIOSAURUS

Large paddles enabled Pliosaurus to speed through the water

PLANTS

THERE MAY BE as many as 375,000 species of plants in the world, from tiny mosses to massive trees higher than houses. Plants and trees are found growing in all habitats, from frozen tundra to hot deserts and under the sea.

LARGEST FLOWER
The giant rafflesia is 105 cm (41 in) across, wider than a car tyre. It weighs 7 kg (15 lb)

PLANT RECORDS

Oldest plant
A holly-like bush in Tasmania is thought to have been growing for more than 43,000 years.

Deadliest fungus
The death cap fungus can kill in minutes.

Largest fruiting body
The fruit of the giant puffball fungus has a 2-m (7-ft) circumference.

Giant puffball is larger than a football

GIANT PUFFBALL

Smelliest flower
To attract insects for pollination, the giant rafflesia flower smells of stinking, rotten meat – a tasty meal for flies!

Biggest cactus
In the deserts of Mexico and the USA, giant saguaro cacti grow 17 m (56 ft) tall. Most of their weight is water.

Largest seed
The huge seed of the coco de mer palm can weigh 25 kg (55 lb), as much as 30 coconuts!

Smallest seed
It would take about 25,000 million tiny orchid seeds to fill a tablespoon.

Fastest grower
Some species of bamboo grow 90 cm (35 in) in a day. The Pacific giant kelp seaweed grows 45 cm (18 in) a day.

Slowest grower
To survive the cold, Antarctic lichens can take up to 100 years to cover a postage-stamp-sized patch of rock.

Longest fronds
Fronds of the Pacific giant kelp seaweed can grow as long as 60 m (197 ft).

Deepest roots
A fig tree growing in South Africa has roots that reach 120 m (394 ft) into the soil.

LEAF RECORDS

Largest leaf
The raffia and bamboo palms both have leaves up to 20 m (66 ft) long.

Smallest leaf
The leaves of the floating duckweed are smaller than a full stop.

Most leaves
A large oak tree may have more than 250,000 leaves.

Largest lily pad
Carried by air-filled ribs, giant water lily leaves are 2.5 m (8 ft) wide.

The leaves of the giant water lily are the weight of a baby

GIANT WATER LILY

TREE RECORDS

Largest tree
"General Sherman", a sequoia tree, weighs an estimated 2,000 tonnes (1,968 tons).

Tallest tree
A coast redwood in Redwood National Park, California, USA, stands 111.25 m (365 ft) tall.

Oldest tree
A bristlecone pine tree in California, USA, is about 4,700 years old.

Largest forest
North Russia's conifers cover 11,000,000 sq km (4,200,000 sq miles).

Largest rainforest
The Amazon rainforest covers 3.3 billion sq km (1.3 billion sq miles).

Most drought resistant
The African baobab tree stores up to 136,000 litres (300,000 gallons) of water in its trunk for use in times of drought.

COAST REDWOOD

INSECTS

THERE ARE AT LEAST one million species of insect, more than all other animal species combined. Most insects have wings, but all have six legs and three body sections.

Bee collects pollen on its back legs

HONEY BEE FERTILIZING FLOWER

BEE AND WASP RECORDS

Largest bee
Wallace's giant bees are as long as your thumb, at 3.9 cm (1½ in).

Smallest bee
Trigona duckei bees are just 2 mm (1/16 in) long.

Smallest wasp
Adult fairyfly wasps are smaller than a pinhead.

Largest wasp
Tarantula-eating hawk moth wasps grow up to 6.7 cm (2⅝ in) long.

Most useful insect
Bees fertilize flowers with pollen, and produce sweet honey.

RECORD WINGS

Smallest moth
The tiny *Stigmella ridiculosa* moth from the Canary Islands has a wingspan of just 2 mm (1/16 in).

Longest migration
Every year, millions of monarch butterflies fly 3,000 km (1,864 miles) from southern Canada and northern USA to their winter roosts in Mexico and California.

Fastest flyer
An Australian dragonfly can dart along at speeds of an amazing 58 km/h (36 mph), but only for short bursts.

Largest wingspan
Earth's rarest butterfly, the Queen Alexandra's birdwing, can measure 28 cm (11 in) between wing tips.

Male has brightly coloured wings

QUEEN ALEXANDRA'S BIRDWING

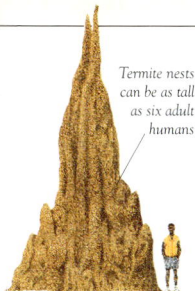

Termite nests can be as tall as six adult humans

TERMITE TOWER
Colonies of tiny insects called termites build huge, towering nests from mud and saliva. African termites' nests can be up to 12.8 m (42 ft) high, the tallest in the insect world.

MORE INSECT RECORDS

Longest insect
Giant stick insects can measure up to 50 cm (20 in) – four times the height of this page.

Highest jumper
Fleas leap 30 cm (12 in) into the air, about 200 times their own height.

Longest jumper
A desert locust can jump 50 cm (20 in), ten times its length.

Loudest insect
Male cicadas' mating songs can be heard 400 m (1,313 ft) away.

Toughest insect
Snow fleas can live in temperatures as low as -15°C (5°F).

Greediest insect
In just eight weeks, a polyphemus moth larva eats 86,000 times its weight in leaves.

Shortest lifespan
After two or three years, mayfly larvae hatch into flies, but die in an hour.

Most dangerous insect
Mosquitoes infect and kill two million people with malaria every year.

BEETLE RECORDS

Heaviest beetle
The gigantic goliath beetle can weigh up to 110 g (4 oz), nearly as heavy as an apple.

Most poisonous beetle
African leaf beetle pupae contain a deadly poison used locally to tip hunting arrows.

Longest living beetle
South American jewel beetles live for 30 years.

RHINOCEROS BEETLE

Horn-like jaws used for fighting other males

Strongest beetle
Rhinoceros and Atlas beetles are so strong they can carry more than 800 times their own weight on their backs.

The rhinoceros beetle is twice this size in life

ARACHNIDS

THERE ARE 73,000 species of
arachnids, which include spiders,
scorpions, ticks, and mites. You
can tell arachnids from insects
as they have eight legs, not six,
and two body parts, not three.

SPIDER RECORDS

Largest spider
With a leg span of 28 cm
(11 in), the Goliath
bird-eating spider from
South America can
cover a dinner plate.

GOLIATH BIRD-EATING SPIDER

Smallest spider
Western Samoan midget
spiders are microscopic.

Smallest web
Midget spider's webs
are 10 mm (⅓ in) across
– the size of a fingernail.

Largest web
Webs made by the orb
weaver spider family
can be 3 m (10 ft) wide
– as large as bedsheets.

Strongest silk
Golden orb spider's silk
is as fine as human hair
but stronger than steel.

Most poisonous spider
Brazilian wandering
spiders are poisonous,
but rarely bite humans.

Fastest runner
For just a few seconds,
house spiders run at
1.9 km/h (1 mph).

ARACHNID RECORDS

Smallest arachnid
Gall mites, which live
inside plant cells, are
only just visible.

Most deadly scorpion
The sting of the Israeli
gold scorpion is the
most poisonous.

Largest scorpion
From its pincers to its
sting, the *Heterometrus
swannerdami* scorpion
measures 18 cm (7 in).

Smallest scorpion
Microbothus pusillus is
13 mm (½ in) long.

*All scorpions
have pincer-like
claws for
seizing
prey*

SCORPION

MOLLUSCS AND CRUSTACEANS

SOFT-BODIED molluscs include octopuses, squid, slugs, and snails. Crustaceans are mainly water-dwellers such as crabs and shrimps, all with a tough protective shell.

Garden snail is tiny in comparison

LARGEST GASTROPOD
The giant African land snail grows 39 cm (15 in) from head to tail.

MOLLUSC RECORDS

Most venomous
The painless bite of the blue-ringed octopus may seem harmless, but it can kill you.

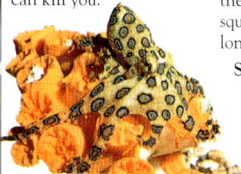

BLUE-RINGED OCTOPUS

Largest mollusc
The world's largest invertebrate (animal without a backbone), the Atlantic giant squid, can grow as long as 20 m (66 ft).

Smallest mollusc
The miniscule gastropod called *Ammonicera* is as small as a single granule of sugar.

Largest bivalve mollusc
Weighing more than 300 kg (661 lb), the giant clam is the largest bivalve, or two-shelled mollusc. It is as heavy as three adults!

Heaviest pearl
The biggest pearl ever, the "Pearl of Laotze", came from a giant clam in the Philippines and weighed 6.4 kg (14 lb).

CRUSTACEAN RECORDS

Heaviest crustacean
North Atlantic lobsters weigh 20 kg (44 lb).

Largest numbers
Swarms of shrimp-like krill cover 440 sq km (170 sq miles).

Smallest crustacean
An Alonella flea is as tiny as a grain of salt.

Largest crustacean
The Japanese spider crab has a leg span of almost 4 m (13 ft).

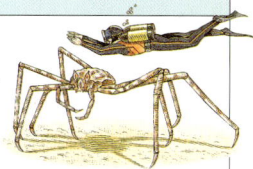

JAPANESE SPIDER CRAB

UNDERWATER LIFE

ABOUT 24,000 FISH species live in the world's fresh and salt waters, with more discovered every year. The oceans are home to a variety of wildlife, from harmless marine creatures to hungry predators.

MOST FEROCIOUS EATER
With their powerful jaws and razor-sharp teeth, piranhas can strip a carcass in minutes

FISH RECORDS

Smallest fish
The tiny Philippino dwarf pygmy goby, which lives in fresh water, has a length of just 8 mm (¼ in).

Longest bony fish
Huge oarfish can measure more than 15 m (49 ft) long.

Most productive fish
The ocean sunfish lays about 300 million tiny eggs, each no bigger than a letter on this page.

Most poisonous to eat
Although the flesh of a death puffer fish is a Japanese delicacy, its liver, blood, and skin are deadly poisonous.

Deepest living fish
Bassogigas fish have been found living at 8,000 m (2,624 ft) deep in the Atlantic Ocean.

Most electric fish
An electric eel from the Amazon River can stun or kill its prey with a powerful electric shock.

Slowest fish
Seahorses are known to be the slowest fish in the ocean. It takes 100 hours to swim just 1.6 km (1 mile).

Fastest fish
Over short distances, the streamlined sailfish can speed through the ocean at more than 100 km/h (62 mph).

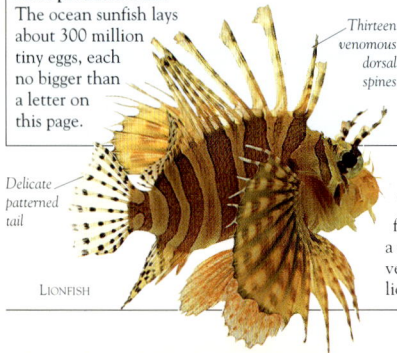

Thirteen venomous dorsal spines

Delicate patterned tail

LIONFISH

POISONOUS FISH
The brightly coloured fins of this lionfish contain a deadly poison. Even more venomous are stonefish, which lie camouflaged on the sea floor.

SHARK RECORDS

Longest shark
The immense whale shark is the largest of all fish, and can grow to lengths of more than 18 m (59 ft).

Smallest shark
With adults reaching just 25 cm (10 in) long, the pygmy shark, also known as the dwarf shark, is the smallest in all the world's oceans.

Largest carnivore
Weighing as much as 0.67 tonne (¼ ton), the enormous great white shark can grow to lengths of 6 m (20 ft) or more.

Sharpest teeth
The great white shark's teeth are 12 cm (5 in) long. As they wear out, new ones replace them.

Most dangerous
Often unfairly blamed, the great white shark is said to attack 50–100 people every year.

Streamlined body enables fast pursuit of prey

Largest egg
The largest known egg, about three times the size of this page, was laid by a whale shark.

Thickest skin
The tough, rubber-like skin of the whale shark is thick, measuring 10 cm (4 in) deep.

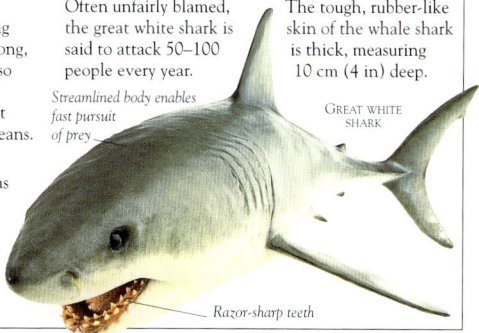

GREAT WHITE SHARK

Razor-sharp teeth

JELLYFISH RECORDS

Most poisonous
A sting from the Australian box jellyfish can prove fatal.

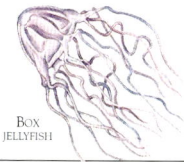

BOX JELLYFISH

Largest jellyfish
The Arctic giant jellyfish has a body of more than 2 m (6 ft) wide and tentacles 36 m (118 ft) long.

Most common
Glass jellyfish live in all oceans, near the surface as well as at depths of 700 m (2,300 ft).

COMMON SUNSTAR

MOST ARMS
Many starfish have 5 arms, but sunstars are known to have between 7 and 13 tentacles!

AMPHIBIANS

INCLUDING FROGS, toads, newts,
and salamanders, amphibians
are found the world over,
except Antarctica. Most can live
both on land and in water, but all
return to water to lay their eggs.

Bright skin warns off predators

TIGER SALAMANDER

NEWT AND SALAMANDER RECORDS

Largest salamander
The largest amphibian,
the Chinese giant
salamander, can grow
more than 1.5 m (5 ft)
long. The Japanese
giant salamander
comes a close second.

Smallest salamander
Tiny Mexican lungless
salamanders are just
14 mm (½ in) long –
that's even smaller
than your little toe!

Hardiest salamander
Northern Russia, where
winter temperatures
can fall as low as -56°C
(-69°F), is home to
Siberian salamanders.
These hardy creatures
often freeze in the soil.

**Largest land
salamander**
The tiger salamander,
which lives on land,
grows to a length of
33 cm (13 in).

**Most poisonous
newt**
The skin, blood,
and muscles of
the Californian
newt contain extremely
powerful nerve poisons
that paralyse enemies.

Spiniest newt
By pushing out its sharp
ribs through its highly
poisonous skin, the
Chinese spiny newt can
fatally stab an attacker.

AFRICAN
BULLFROG

LONGEST FROG
Measuring 90 cm (35 in)
long and weighing 3 kg
(6½ lb), an outstretched
African bullfrog is
longer than your arm!
The Goliath frog is the
second longest, but is
heavier, weighing up
to 4 kg (8¾ lb).

FROG RECORDS

Largest frog
The body of the African Goliath frog measures 30 cm (12 in), while its outstretched legs add another 40 cm (16 in).

Worst smelling frog
The skunk frog from Venezuela defends itself by giving off a terrible smell, similar to that produced by skunks.

Smallest frog
Sminthillus limbatus and *Psyllophryne didactyla* both share the record, each less than 10 mm (⅛ in) in length.

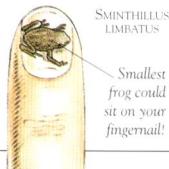

SMINTHILLUS
LIMBATUS

Smallest frog could sit on your fingernail!

Good eyesight is vital for spotting prey

GOLDEN MANATELLA FROG

Brightly-coloured skin warns off predators

Toxic chemicals in skin

Most see-through frog
Through the almost transparent skin on a glass frog's underside, you can see its bones and internal organs.

Largest tadpole
Most tadpoles grow into larger adults, but the 16-cm (6-in) long tadpoles of the paradoxical frog change into tiny adults just a third of the size.

Most poisonous frog
The skin of the poison-dart frog holds enough poison to kill 20,000 mice. Golden manatella frogs of Madagascar contain similar poisons.

Longest jump
In a frog-jumping show held in California, USA, an African sharp-nosed frog leapt an amazing distance of 5.35 m (17½ ft).

TOAD RECORDS

Smallest toad
Bufo taitanus beiranus, a tiny toad found in Africa, is the world's smallest. It has a body length that measures 2.4 cm (1 in), only just bigger than a grape!

Record cane toads
Cane toads lay 35,000 eggs a year, more than any amphibian. Cane toads are also the largest – "The Prince" was 40 cm (16 in) long.

CANE TOAD

REPTILES

SCALY-SKINNED lizards, snakes, turtles, tortoises, and crocodiles lay their eggs on land. As they are cold-blooded, they rely on the Sun for energy and warmth.

KOMODO DRAGON

LIZARD RECORDS

Longest tongue
A chameleon's tongue, "fired" out of its mouth to catch prey, is 1.5 times the length of its body.

Smallest lizard
The Virgin Island gecko is 18 mm (¾ in) long.

GECKO

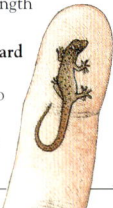

Largest lizard
Male Indonesian Komodo dragons can grow up to 3 m (10 ft) long; females measure about 2 m (6½ ft).

Longest lizard
The total length of the Papuan monitor lizard is 4.75 m (15½ ft), of which almost three-quarters is tail.

Only venomous lizards
American Gila monsters and Mexican beaded lizards are the only venomous ones known.

Only marine lizard
The Galapagos Islands' iguana swims and dives in the ocean, feeding mainly on seaweed.

CROCODILE RECORDS

Largest reptile
The saltwater crocodile grows up to 10 m (33 ft) long. It is also the most dangerous crocodile.

Smallest crocodile
Dwarf caimans from South America rarely grow more than 1.5 m (5 ft) long.

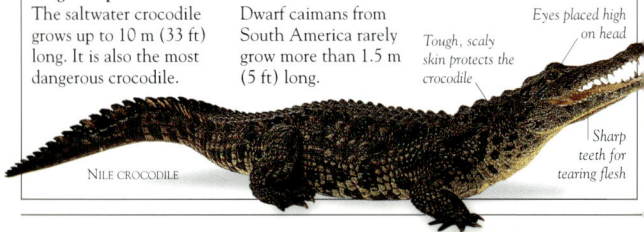

Eyes placed high on head

Tough, scaly skin protects the crocodile

Sharp teeth for tearing flesh

NILE CROCODILE

TURTLE AND TORTOISE RECORDS

Smallest turtle
The stinkpot turtle, so-called because of its terrible smell, measures 8 cm (3 in) in length.

Oldest tortoise
A Marion's tortoise was more than 150 years old when it was killed accidentally in 1918.

Slowest tortoise
Even a hungry tortoise's top speed is only ⅕ km/h (⅛ mph).

Largest tortoise
Giant tortoises in the Galapagos Islands can measure 1.4 m (4½ ft) long.

GALAPAGOS GIANT TORTOISE

SNAKE RECORDS

Longest snake
A reticulated python from Indonesia measured 10 m (33 ft) in length, almost half as long as a tennis court.

Heaviest snake
The massive anaconda from South America is probably the world's most weighty snake, tipping the scales at 200 kg (440 lb).

Most venomous snakes
About 700 species of snake are poisonous, but sea snakes are the most venomous of all.

Shortest snake
Pencil-thin thread snakes grow just 10 cm (4 in) long.

Longest fangs
The deadly gaboon viper, found in Africa, has extremely long fangs, measuring up to 5 cm (2 in) in length.

Longest fast
After a good meal, snakes can go for months before eating again. The record is just over three years.

Front fangs inject prey with a toxic venom

Body coiled ready for attack

Most dangerous snakes on land
Between them, Asian cobras, vipers, and kraits are responsible for more human deaths by snakebite every year than any other snakes.

Largest meal ever eaten
A hungry rock python managed to swallow an impala (a kind of antelope), whole!

Cobras expand their "hood" by raising the ribs in the neck

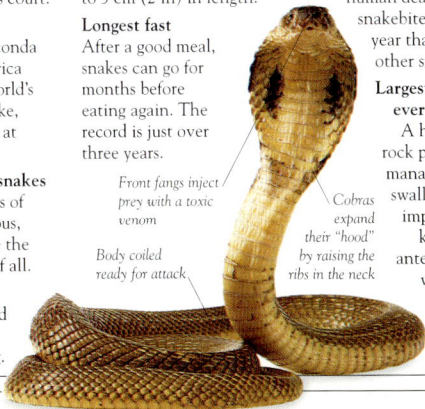

THAI COBRA

BIRDS

THERE ARE MORE than 9,000 species of bird, ranging from tiny hummingbirds to long-legged ostriches. All birds have feathers and wings, and most can fly, though not all.

FIRST BIRD
Archaeopteryx
lived about 150
million years ago.

FLYING RECORDS

Furthest flight
Each year, the Arctic tern flies 40,000 km (25,000 miles) from the Arctic to the Antarctic and back again.

Most aerial bird
Sooty terns spend up to four years airborne before landing to breed.

Fastest diver
As it dives on prey in mid-air, a peregrine falcon can reach speeds of 180 km/h (112 mph).

Slowest flying bird
American and Eurasian woodcocks can fly at speeds of just 8 km/h (5 mph) when courting.

Highest flying bird
Some Ruppell griffon vultures fly at heights of 11,300 m (37,000 ft) – as high as an airliner.

Fastest flying bird
Reaching speeds of 171 km/h (106 mph), the spine-tail swift is the fastest level flyer.

NEST AND EGG RECORDS

Smallest nest
The nest of the vervain hummingbird is about the size of half a walnut.

Largest nest
A huge nest built by bald eagles weighed 3 tonnes (2.9 tons), as much as three cars.

OSTRICH AND
HUMMINGBIRD
EGGS

*Smallest
eggs weigh
0.25g
(⅟₁₀₀ oz)*

Smallest eggs
The miniscule eggs of the bee hummingbird are as small as peas.

Largest eggs
Eggs laid by ostriches can be up to 20 cm (8 in) long and weigh about 1.65 kg (3½ lb).

*Ostriches
have long legs
to help them
run fast*

LARGEST BIRD
The ostrich can grow to 2.7 m (9 ft) tall and weigh 156 kg (344 lb). It cannot fly but runs very fast.

*Stiff, narrow wings
are used as flippers
to propel the penguin
through the water*

FASTEST SWIMMING BIRDS
Penguins are superb swimmers and divers. The fastest swimmer, the gentoo, speeds along at 27 km/h (17 mph).

BIRD RECORDS

Rarest bird
There is now only one surviving Spix's macaw left in the wild because of trapping for the pet trade.

Longest bill
The bill of the Australian pelican can reach a length of up to 47 cm (18½ in), the length of your arm from elbow to fingertip! It holds more food than the pelican's stomach!

Longest feathers
The tail feathers of the phoenix fowl from Japan can measure as long as 10 m (33 ft).

Most feathers
Swans and other large birds have more than 25,000 feathers, three-quarters of which are on the head and neck.

Smallest bird
About the size of a large butterfly, a male bee hummingbird weighs as little as 1.6 g (⅛ oz) and is 57 mm (2¼ in) in length.

*Wings measure
3.6 m (12 ft)
from tip to tip*

WANDERING
ALBATROSS

Longest wings
The wandering albatross has the longest wingspan of any bird, stretching out as wide as a small car.

Heaviest flying bird
Kori bustards weigh up to 18 kg (40 lb). Above this weight, muscles cannot grow strong enough for flight.

Only poisonous bird
The New Guinea hooded pitohui's skin, wings, and internal organs contain strong poisons if eaten.

LAND MAMMALS

RANGING IN SIZE from tiny bats to long-necked giraffes, land mammals are warm-blooded creatures that, uniquely, feed their young on milk. They live all over the world, from the icy Arctic to tropical rainforests.

SLEEPIEST MAMMAL
The sloth spends up to 20 hours a day dozing whilst its claws cling to a branch.

The tallest and largest land mammals dwarf an average human

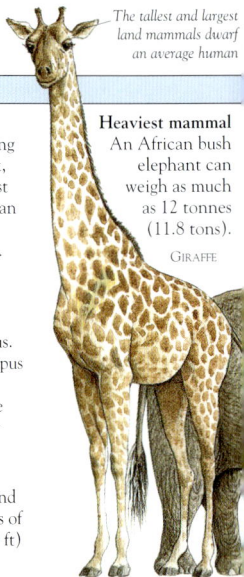

LAND MAMMAL RECORDS

Largest land mammal
The awesome male African elephant can grow a record-breaking 3–4 m (10–13 ft) in height and at least 5 m (16½ ft) in length.

Smallest mammal
Kitti's hog-nosed bat has a weight of just 1.5 g (¹⁄₂₀ oz). It is only about the size of a large bumblebee.

Hog-nosed bat is only slightly larger than this in life

HOG-NOSED BAT

Tallest mammal
With its extremely long legs and graceful neck, the giraffe is the tallest mammal on land. It can grow to 6 m (19½ ft), as tall as three people.

Most poisonous mammal
Only two types of mammal are poisonous. The duck-billed platypus has poisonous spurs on its back legs. Some shrews have a slightly poisonous bite.

Highest living
Wild yaks in China and Tibet climb to heights of over 6,000 m (20,000 ft) in search of food.

Heaviest mammal
An African bush elephant can weigh as much as 12 tonnes (11.8 tons).

GIRAFFE

MARSUPIAL RECORDS

Largest marsupial
The male red kangaroo can grow more than 2 m (6½ ft) tall and 2.5 m (8 ft) in overall length.

Highest jumper
A red kangaroo once leapt over a pile of timber 3 m (10 ft) high to escape from a pack of hunting dogs.

Smallest marsupial
The rare long-tailed planigale is about the same size as a small mouse.

Fastest grower
A baby kangaroo, or joey, is the size of a thimble, but as it matures it grows by 30,000 times!

KANGAROO AND JOEY

Joey is pictured actual size

Longest gestation
The pregnancy of an Asian elephant lasts 660 days, about 22 months, more than twice that of a human mother.

AFRICAN ELEPHANT

Fastest on land
Over short distances, a cheetah can race along at speeds of 100 km/h (62 mph). Its claws grip the ground like the spikes of running shoes to give it amazing acceleration.

Largest herds
In the 19th century, some herds of springbok in South Africa were so enormous they took three days to pass a given point.

Longest hibernation
The barrow ground squirrel of Alaska, USA, hibernates for nine months at a time.

Longest lifespan
Humans are the longest-lived mammals, but Asian elephants come a close second. The oldest known died aged 78.

Most endangered
It is estimated that one species dies out every 15 minutes. Among those most endangered mammals are the giant panda, the Javan rhinoceros, and the woolly spider monkey.

Largest carnivore
Gentle-looking polar bears are in fact seal-eating carnivores that can weigh more than 1 tonne (⅞ ton).

More land mammal records

There are 4,000 different species of mammal, and 19 groups. Rodents make up the largest group, with about 1,750 species, followed by bats, of which there are 950 species.

ON ITS OWN
The nocturnal aardvark of Africa is the only living member of its order. It lives in a burrow.

AARDVARK

RODENT RECORDS

Largest rodent
The capybara of South America weighs up to 66 kg (145 lb). It is about the same size as a sheep.

Smallest rodent
The tiny pygmy jerboa of Pakistan only grows about 14 cm (5½ in) long, of which 9.5 cm (3¾ in) is tail. For its small size it has enormous back feet, that measure almost 2 cm (¾ in) long. The jerboa uses them for jumping.

Most dangerous rodent
In medieval times, an outbreak of plague, the "Black Death", killed a quarter of Europe's population in just four years. The disease came from fleas that lived on black rats.

PRIMATE RECORDS

Most colourful primate
The face and bottom of the male mandrill, a baboon, are unusual because they are bright scarlet and blue, to warn off rivals.

Loudest primate
The deafening dawn chorus of the howler monkey, warning enemies to keep away, can be heard from at least 3 km (2 miles).

Smallest primate
The tiny western rufous mouse lemur from Madagascar is about the size of a hamster but it has a long tail.

Largest primate
The adult male gorilla stands 2 m (6½ ft) tall, weighing up to 200 kg (440 lb).

Sturdy arms and legs to support body weight

GORILLA

Domestic animals

Mammals that are kept by humans are called domestic animals. Dogs were first tamed about 12,000 years ago. Today, many different animals are kept as pets.

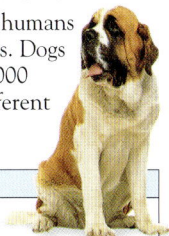

ST BERNARD

CAT AND DOG RECORDS

First pet cat
Pet cats were treated as sacred by Egyptians some 3,500 years ago.

RAGDOLL

Smallest cat
Singapuras weigh 1.8 kg (4 lb).

Largest cat
A ragdoll cat is twice the size of an average pet cat.

Largest dog
The St Bernard weighs 77–91 kg (170–200 lb).

Tallest dog
A Great Dane can stand 1 m (3 ft) high at the shoulder, about three times taller than the smallest falabella horse.

Smallest dog
A tiny chihuahua is as light as 0.45 kg (1 lb).

HORSE RECORDS

Largest horse
Shire horses are the tallest and heaviest. The largest on record stood more than 2 m (6½ ft) tall and weighed 1.5 tonnes (1¼ tons).

Fastest horse
In Mexico, 1945, a racehorse called "Big Racket" ran at a record-breaking speed of 69.6 km/h (43⅓ mph).

Strongest horse
A pair of shire horses can easily pull a load of 50 tonnes (49 tons), equivalent to a large lorry and its full trailer.

Smallest horse
Falabellas from Argentina stand only 40 cm (16 in) tall, about the height of a small dog.

FALABELLA

PET RECORDS

Most common pet
Cats and dogs prove most popular with pet lovers the world over.

Fastest breeders
Female common rabbits can give birth to at least 20 young every year.

Most popular bird
The budgerigar is one of the most common caged birds.

Oldest gerbil
A gerbil lived with its owner in Michigan, USA, for eight years.

Spotted coat can have five patterns

SEA MAMMALS

OF THE 4,000 mammal species, about 120 live in the sea. They include cetaceans (porpoises, whales, and dolphins), pinnipeds (seals and walruses), and sirenians (manatees and dugongs).

LARGEST MOUTH
The gigantic blue whale has the largest mouth of all animals. These tall jaw bones come from one of the last blue whales ever caught and are erected in the seaside town of Whitby, UK.

BLUE WHALE

Blue whales tip the scales at 120 tonnes (118 tons)

WHALE AND DOLPHIN RECORDS

Largest
The blue whale is the largest animal alive today, measuring at least 33.5 m (110 ft) long. On land it would be squashed by its weight.

Fastest
Killer whales are the speediest sea mammals, swimming at up to 55 km/h (34 mph).

Loudest
Blue whales are also the loudest sea mammals. Their "songs" register 188 decibels and can be heard 850 km (528 miles) away.

Longest song
The humpback whale's "song" lasts for half an hour and contains many different tones.

Thickest blubber
When feeding, a right whale's blubber, or fat beneath the skin, can have a thickness of as much as 60 cm (2 ft). It protects the whale from the cold.

Longest lived
It is thought that fin whales reach a grand old age of 90–100 years.

PINNIPED RECORDS

Largest
The southern elephant seal is enormous. Males can grow up to 6.5 m (21 ft) long and weigh 4 tonnes (⁴⁄₁₀ tons).

Rarest
It is estimated that there may be as few as 500 wild Mediterranean monk seals left.

Fastest
For short bursts only, Californian sea lions can swim through the water at speeds of up to 40 km/h (25 mph).

Longest whiskers
A male Antarctic fur seal was found to have whiskers that had grown an amazing 50 cm (20 in) in length.

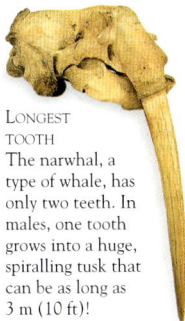

LONGEST TOOTH
The narwhal, a type of whale, has only two teeth. In males, one tooth grows into a huge, spiralling tusk that can be as long as 3 m (10 ft)!

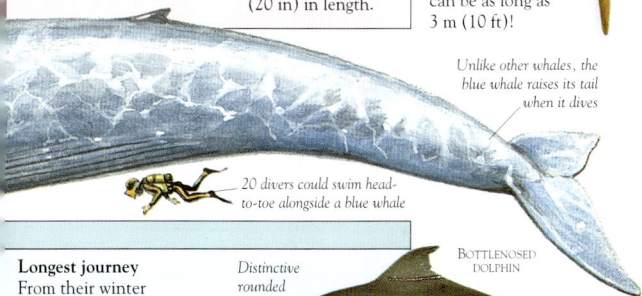

Unlike other whales, the blue whale raises its tail when it dives

20 divers could swim head-to-toe alongside a blue whale

Longest journey
From their winter breeding grounds in Mexico to their summer feeding grounds in the Bering Sea, grey whales swim up to 20,000 km (12,500 miles) a year.

Tallest blow
The blue whale's blow reaches 12 m (39 ft), as high as six tall people.

Distinctive rounded nose

BOTTLENOSED DOLPHIN

Deepest diver
Sperm whales can dive to depths of more than 2,000 m (6,561 ft).

MOST FAMOUS DOLPHIN
Historically, dolphins and people have had a special relationship. In the well-known TV show *Flipper*, a bottlenosed dolphin and a young boy become friends.

HUMAN BODY

AN AMAZINGLY COMPLEX machine, the human body is made up of hundreds of working parts. Each cell, organ, nerve, bone, and muscle has a vital job to do to keep you alive and healthy.

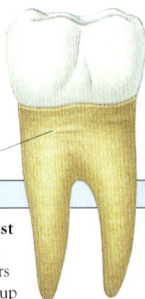

Tooth shown actual size

BONE AND TEETH RECORDS

Longest bone
Your femurs, or thighbones, measure about a quarter of your overall height.

Smallest bone
The tiny stirrup-shaped bone inside your middle ear is only about 3 mm (⅛ in) long, about the size of a grain of rice.

Largest joint
Your strong knee joints help to bear the body's weight and work like hinges to bend the legs.

Smallest joint
The tiny joints between the hammer, anvil, and stirrup bones in your ears are the smallest in your body.

Biggest tooth
Molars grow up to 4 cm (1½ in) long. The four back molars are known as wisdom teeth.

MOLAR

Hardest substance
Tough white enamel coats all your teeth.

HEART AND BLOOD RECORDS

Largest artery
The aorta, which carries blood from your heart to your body, is thicker than your thumb, at about 2.5 cm (1 in).

Largest vein
The inferior vena cava carries blood back from the body to your heart.

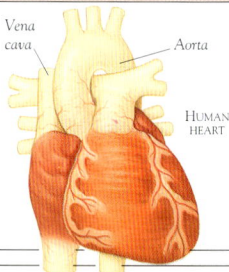

Vena cava

Aorta

HUMAN HEART

First heart transplant
Skilled South African surgeon Christiaan Barnard performed a heart transplant in December 1967.

Most common blood
Almost half of all the world's people belong to blood group O.

MUSCLE RECORDS

Largest muscle
Your buttock and thigh muscles are called *Gluteus maximus*.

Strongest muscle
The masseter muscles in the sides of your jaw have to be strong because they help you to bite and chew.

Fastest muscle
The hard-working muscles in your eyelids make your eyes blink 15 times every minute!

CELL RECORDS

Largest cell
The female egg cell, or ovum, can just be seen without a microscope.

Smallest cell
Measuring just 0.005 mm ($\frac{1}{5000}$ in) across, the smallest cells are in the cerebellum part of your brain.

Longest-lived cell
The 15 billion cells in your brain can last for your whole lifetime.

Shortest-lived cell
The cells that line the small intestine only live for 2 to 3 days.

Fastest-dividing cells
Cells divide at the fastest rate during a baby's development in the womb.

The thinnest skin, on your eyelids, is 0.5 mm ($\frac{1}{50}$ in) thick

The shoulder joint is the most flexible

The sartorius muscle, which runs from the pelvis to just below the knee, is the longest

Loudest voice measured 119 decibels, louder than a rock concert

Skin is your largest organ, covering your whole body. It has a surface area of 2 m² (22 ft²)

Fingertips contain thousands of sense receptors, making them the most sensitive part of your body

The sciatic nerve is the body's longest. It runs from the base of the spine to the knee

The thickest skin is on the soles of your feet. It is 6 mm ($\frac{1}{4}$ in) thick

HUMAN BODY

PEOPLE AND SOCIETY

Most highly populated city: Tokyo, Japan

COUNTRIES, CITIES, AND TOWNS

OF THE 5.7 BILLION people in the world, about half live in cities. The rapid growth of the world's population is a major problem facing many nations, especially poor countries.

CONTINENT AND COUNTRY RECORDS

Largest continent
Asia is the biggest of the seven continents, covering about 44,390,000 sq km (17,139,000 sq miles).

Smallest continent
Australia has an area of 7,868,810 sq km (2,967,877 sq miles).

Largest country
Russia spreads over 17,070,289 sq km (6,590,876 sq miles).

Smallest country
The Vatican City in Italy is just 0.44 sq km (⅛ sq miles).

Most neighbours
China has borders with no less than 16 other nations.

Country with longest name
Libya's official name is al-Jamahiriyah al-Arabiya al-Libiyah ash-Shabiyah al-Ishirakiyah.

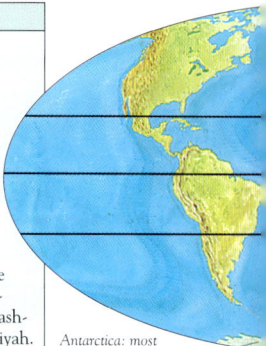

Antarctica: most sparsely populated

CITY AND TOWN RECORDS

First town
Built just before 8000 BC, the flourishing settlement at Jericho in the Jordan Valley, Israel, was probably the world's first town.

Oldest capital city
Lying on the banks of the River Barada, Syria's ancient capital city, Damascus, has been inhabited since about 2500 BC.

JERICHO STONE TOWER

Protective wall and ditch built all around Jericho town

POPULATION RECORDS

Highest population
One in every five people in the world lives in China – a population of 1,200 million. India comes in second place, home to 950 million people.

Russia: largest country

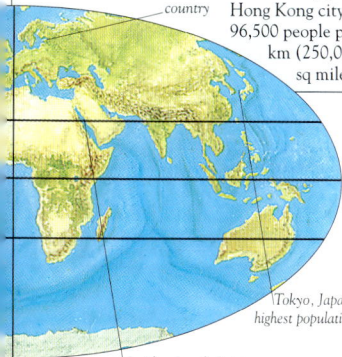

Smallest population
Just a thousand people live in Vatican City, home to the Pope.

Highest city population
Tokyo has a population of more than 27 million.

Densest city population
Hong Kong city has 96,500 people per sq km (250,000 per sq mile).

Sparsest population
Antarctica is only inhabited by scientists – one for every 3,550 sq km (1,325 sq miles).

Highest birth rate
In Rwanda, 58,000 babies are born yearly.

Lowest birth rate
In Italy, 10,000 babies are born annually.

TOP POPULATIONS
This chart shows the percentage of people living on each continent. Asia is home to the majority.

ASIA 63%

AFRICA 12.5%

AUSTRALASIA AND OCEANIA 0.5%

EUROPE 10.4%

ANTARCTICA 0%

SOUTH AMERICA 6.7%

NORTH AMERICA 6.9%

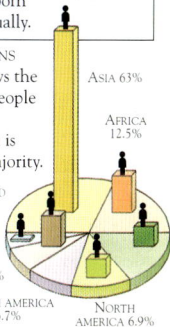

Tokyo, Japan: highest population

Jericho, Israel: first town

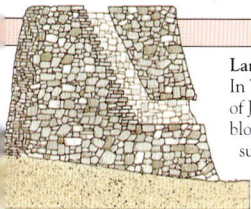

Largest city
In Tokyo, the capital of Japan, shiny office blocks and concrete surburbs make up the largest conurbation in the world.

Highest city
Known as the "roof of the world", Tibet lies high in the Himalayas. Lhasa, its capital, sits 3,684 m (12,087 ft) above sea level.

RULERS AND LEADERS

EACH COUNTRY has a group of people who decide how it should be organized and run. Some countries are ruled by a royal family, headed by a king or queen. Others have a central authority called a government, made up of politicians.

ROMAN EMPEROR
AUGUSTUS

FIRST ROMAN EMPEROR
The Roman leader Augustus was the first to rule under the title of "Emperor". He governed the newly formed Roman Empire from 27 BC–AD 14, a time of great prosperity.

MONARCH RECORDS

Longest reign
King Louis XIV (r.1643–1715) of France reigned for a total of 72 years, during which time France became the most powerful country in Europe. Louis was only five years old when he came to the throne.

Longest reign in the ancient world
Pharaoh Pepy II is said to have ruled Egypt for about 94 years, beginning in 2281 BC, at the age of just six years.

Longest present reign
Bhumibol Adulyadej, the King of Thailand, came to the throne in June 1946 and still reigns over the country.

Shortest reign ever
Crown Prince Luis Filipe of Portugal was king for only 20 minutes on 1st February 1908 before he was shot and fatally wounded.

Longest reigning queen
The world's longest reigning queen was Victoria. She ruled Britain from 1837 to 1901, a total of 63 years, during which she presided over a growing colonial empire.

Most children
The Egyptian pharaoh, Ramesses II (r. 1289–1224 BC) had his own harem by the time he was ten, resulting in a record 111 sons and 67 daughters!

BUST OF
PERIKLES,
ATHENIAN
LEADER

FIRST DEMOCRACY
Greek men received rights 2,500 years ago to vote in the world's first democracy. Perikles, leader from 443–429 BC, allowed free speech.

WORLD HEADS OF STATE RECORDS

Longest serving president
General Suharto of Indonesia took office in 1967 and is still president of the country.

Longest serving prime minister
Prime Minister Khalifa bin Sulman al-Khalifa of Bahrain, has been in office since 1969.

First female president
Maria Estela Peron of Argentina held office from 1974 to 1975.

First female prime minister
Sri Lanka's Sirimavo Bandaranaike served from 1960 to 1964 and between 1970 and 1977.

Oldest prime minister
Morocco's Grand Vizier, El Hadji Muhammad el Mokri, is said to have died aged 112 years.

Youngest prime minister
Dr Mario Frick, 28, of Liechtenstein was appointed in 1993.

ELECTION RECORDS

First vote for women
Women of New Zealand won the vote in 1893, while those on the Isle of Man, UK, could vote in 1880.

Largest electorate
In India's 1991 elections, more than 315 million people out of the 489 million eligible cast their vote.

Highest majority
In the 1989 Soviet elections, Boris Yeltsin gained 5,118,745 of the 5,722,937 votes in Moscow.

Largest ballot paper
For Prague's 1994 municipal elections, a ballot paper the size of a bed sheet was required to list 1,187 candidates.

US PRESIDENT RECORDS

First
George Washington, the first US president, held office from 1789–1797.

Longest serving
Franklin D. Roosevelt served as president for 12 years, between 1933–1945.

Last to die in office
John F. Kennedy was assassinated on 22 November 1963, having served less than three years.

GEORGE WASHINGTON

EXPLORATION AND TRAVEL

SINCE ANCIENT TIMES, when little was
known of the world, improved maps,
instruments, and transport have led
explorers and traders to new
lands. Research and adventure
inspire modern explorers.

FIRST MAP
A map
drawn on
a clay tablet in 2300 BC shows
Babylon at the centre of the Earth.

EXPLORATION FIRSTS

COOK'S SHIP
ENDEAVOUR

First to explore Pacific
The Polynesians first
explored the Pacific
Ocean more than
2,000 years ago.

**First European
to map the Pacific**
James Cook
(UK) drew
a map of the
Pacific Ocean
based on his
expeditions
between
1768–1776.

**First around
the globe**
In 1519–1522
Portuguese sailor,
Magellan, headed
a global voyage.
He was killed on
the way home.

**First European
to reach America**
Christopher Columbus
is credited with landing
in North America in
1492, the first European
to do so. But the Viking
Leif Erikson may have
beaten him to it,
in the 11th century.

First to cross Australia
Americans Burke and
Wills crossed Australia
from south to north in
1860, but both died on
the return journey.

First to climb Everest
On 29 May 1953,
Sherpa Tenzing Norgay
and Edmund Hillary
reached the summit
of Mount Everest, the
world's highest peak.

NAVIGATION RECORDS

First compass
The magnetic compass, which revolutionized navigation, dates from 11th-century China.

First mariner's astrolabe
In the 1470s, the astrolabe (circular map of the sky) was adapted for use at sea.

FIRST COMPASS

First octant
Invented in 1731, the octant is used to calculate latitude (the distance north or south of the Equator).

Sextant measures latitude to 0.01 of a degree

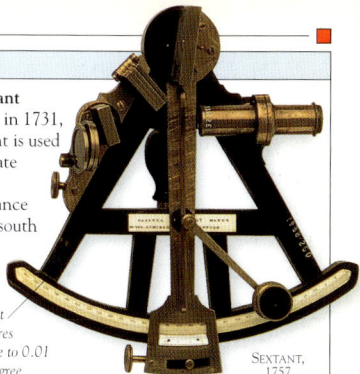

SEXTANT, 1757

First sextant
English inventor John Campbell designed the sextant in 1757. It is still one of the basic tools of navigation.

First sea chronometer
Used for measuring longitude (distance east or west), chronometers were invented in 1759 by John Harrison, UK.

POLAR EXPLORATION RECORDS

First to the North Pole
Robert Peary from the USA claimed to have reached the North Pole in 1909. Doubts still remain about his claim.

First to the South Pole
Norwegian explorer, Roald Amundsen reached the South Pole on 14 December 1911 after a 53-day march.

First snowmobile
British Robert Scott's motorized sledge was the forerunner of modern snowmobiles.

First to both Poles
In 1952, Crary, USA, flew to the North Pole. He took a snowmobile to the South Pole in 1961.

ADMUNDSEN'S TEAM

Dog sleds were the key to Amundsen's success

FOOD AND FARMING

UNTIL ABOUT 10,000 years ago, people lived a nomadic lifestyle, hunting and gathering their food. Gradually, they began to settle in one place and to cultivate crops on the land and domesticate wild animals.

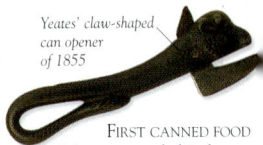

Yeates' claw-shaped can opener of 1855

FIRST CANNED FOOD
A hammer and chisel were used to open the first canned food in 1811! It was another 44 years before can openers appeared.

FOOD AND DRINK FIRSTS

Burger in bread bun: fast food of the 20th century

HAMBURGER

First hamburger
Hamburgers are named after Hamburg, Germany, where they originated in the 1890s.

First potatoes
South American potatoes were brought to Europe by Spanish explorers in Peru.

First sandwich
The UK's Earl of Sandwich asked for bread and ham as a convenient snack when gambling.

First chewing gum
Adams, USA, used the plant sap chicle to make chewing gum.

First tea
Tea, first grown in east Asia, became popular in the 17th century.

First champagne
Don Pérignon, a French monk, first made champagne in 1670.

First Coca-cola
In 1886, USA's John Pemberton invented the most successful soft drink, Coca-Cola.

RECORD CONSUMERS

Top calorie consumers
The Irish have a daily calorie intake of 3,952.

Greatest chocaholics
Americans eat 600,000 tonnes (590,520 tons) of cocoa every year.

Sweetest teeth
In Cuba, 89 kg (197 lb) of sugar are used yearly.

Top beer drinkers
Germans drink an average 142 litres (250 pints) of beer annually.

Ice lovers
On average, each American eats 2 litres (4 pints) of ice-cream per year.

ICE-CREAM

FARMING HISTORY RECORDS

First plough
In Mesopotamia, 3500 BC, the first ploughs worked with a weighted hoe attached to an ox, which pulled them.

Oxen attached here

WOODEN PLOUGH, 1763

Mouldboard lifts and turns soil

First reaping machine
Scotsman Patrick Bell was the first to develop a mechanical reaping machine in 1826.

First combine harvester
Built in the USA in 1838, the first combine harvester was pulled by 30 mules. It was the brainchild of Hascall and Moore.

RECORD ANNUAL CROP PRODUCERS

Orange grower
Brazil grows 20 million tonnes (tons) of oranges each year.

Apple grower
About five million tonnes (tons) of apples from America are picked and sold worldwide annually.

Banana grower
India farms seven million tonnes (tons) of bananas yearly.

Plantain grower
Uganda is the world's top plantain producer, harvesting about eight million tonnes (tons) every year.

WHEAT

Potato grower
Russia's soils yield loads of potatoes weighing 37.8 million tonnes (tons) each year.

Wheat grower
Per year, China reaps 100 million tonnes (tons) of wheat.

Rice grower
The top rice farmer, China annually grows 188 million tonnes (tons).

Beet grower
France grows some 31 million tonnes (tons) of sugar beet in a year.

LIVESTOCK RECORDS

Most common
There are 11,000 million chickens in the world, of which 2,000 million live in China.

Most cattle
India is home to about 192 million cattle, more than any other country.

Most sheep
More than 146 million sheep graze the pastures of Australia.

SHEEP

TRADE AND INDUSTRY

EARLY TRADE began with people bartering their excess crops or animals for other items they needed. Today, industries small and large operate all around the world, employing millions of people and handling vast amounts of goods.

EARLY MONEY
Cowrie shells were used as money in China 3,500 years ago and have been found in India, Africa, and Asia.

MONEY RECORDS

LYDIAN ONE STATER COINS

Hammered punches

First coins
The first coins were minted in Lydia (now Turkey) in about 600 BC. They were stamped with the king's lion seal.

First paper money
The Chinese were the first to use paper money in about the 11th century AD to replace their heavy iron coins.

First credit card
Launched in the USA in 1950, the *Diners Club* card was the first credit card. It was introduced to allow people to pay for restaurant meals.

First smartcard
The French *Carte Bleu* was the first credit card with a built-in computer to record transactions.

CHINESE PAPER MONEY, 14TH CENTURY

World's richest person
With a fortune estimated at about $25,000 million, the Sultan of Brunei is believed to be the world's richest man.

CREDIT IDENTIFICATION CARD

the Diners' Club

SIGNATURE

EXPIRES JUNE 30, 1951
SUBJECT TO TERMS OF REVERSE SIDE

DINERS CLUB CARD

WORLD COMMERCE RECORDS

First traders
Phoenicians were trading metals, cloth, and animals with the Mediterranean peoples from about 3000 BC.

First common market
In 1968, the European Economic Community (EEC) stopped trade tariffs for members.

Largest company
General Motors, based in Detroit, USA, and worldwide, produces about 2 million cars every year, employs 745,000 people, and announces some of the world's largest profits.

Largest drug company
GlaxoWellcome is a pharmaceutical giant.

Largest food company
Top food company Nestlé's best-seller is *KitKat* – 418 are eaten every second!

Largest importer
Japan imports about 95 per cent of its industrial metals and also buys in coal, oil, and gas.

Largest stock exchange
The New York Stock Exchange is the biggest.

Cars are manuactured on production lines with people and robots manning every stage

GENERAL MOTORS CAR PLANT

EMPLOYMENT RECORDS

Country with most workers
China has a 584,569,000-strong workforce, more than any other country.

Country with most farmers
More than 90 per cent of the people that live in Nepal work as farmers.

Largest employer
About 18 per cent of Indian people work for Indian Railways, which employs 1,602,000 workers. There are 14 levels of ticket clerk!

Longest holidays
In Austria and Belgium, workers have 30 days' holiday a year, more than anywhere else.

Longest strike
When it ended in 1961, a strike involving barbers' assistants in Copenhagen, Denmark had lasted for 33 years.

Lowest unemployment
In December 1973, only 81 people out of a population of 6.6 million in Switzerland did not have jobs.

ENERGY

Transport, industry, and homes use vast amounts of energy. Most of this comes from fossil fuels – coal, oil, and gas. But as supplies run low, renewable energy sources, such as wind, water, and solar power, are becoming more important.

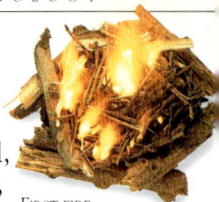

First fire
Charcoal remains of fires dating from 600,000 BC have been found in caves at Choukoutien, China.

FOSSIL FUEL RECORDS

Largest oil producer
Saudi Arabia produces 8,965,000 barrels of oil every day.

Largest gas producer
Some 510 million tonnes (502 million tons) of natural gas are produced annually in Russia.

Largest coal producer
China and the USA each produce 1.6 billion tonnes (1½ billion tons) of coal per year.

Oil strike

Largest oil consumer
The USA uses the equivalent of about 1,800 million tonnes (1,772 million tons) of oil in just one year.

Greatest offshore oil disaster
In July 1988, 167 people were tragically killed on the British Piper Alpha oil production platform in the North Sea.

Worst oil spill
In June 1979, an oil slick measuring 640 km (400 miles) poured into the Gulf of Campeche in the Gulf of Mexico, causing much damage to wildlife and the environment.

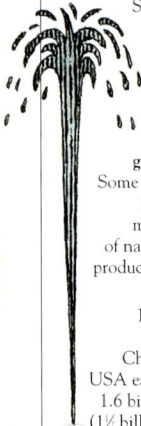

NUCLEAR RECORDS

Most nuclear reactors
The USA has 108 nuclear reactors.

Greatest uranium producer
Every year Canada produces 9,250 tonnes (9,104 tons) of uranium.

Largest power station
Bruce station, Canada, has an output of 6,910 megawatts.

First nuclear reactor
In 1942, Italian Fermi (1901–1954) built the first nuclear reactor.

Worst accident
In 1986, at Chernobyl, Ukraine, an explosion released radioactive material into the air.

First windmill
Windmills, whose sails turned millstones used to grind flour, were made in Persia in about AD 650 and appeared in Europe around AD 1150.

Millstones kept in here

MODEL OF EUROPEAN POST MILL

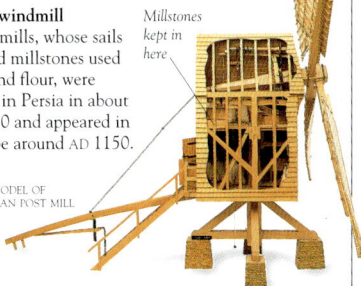

First hydroelectric plant
Hydroelectricity was generated using turbines in an ex-leather mill in England, in 1881.

First wave power
In 1974, Stephen Salter of Scotland devised one of the first practical wave-powered generators.

First wind farm
Built in the USA in 1982, the Goldendale Columbia River Gorge wind-driven turbines generate a million watts.

Largest solar plant
The Harper Lake Site in the Mojave Desert, USA spreads over 518 ha (1,280 acres).

LONGEST BLADES
The blades of the world's largest wind turbines, each up to 50 m (164 ft) long, could fit one hundred people standing side by side.

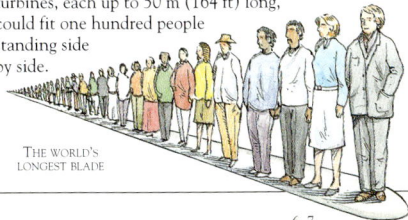

THE WORLD'S LONGEST BLADE

Largest generator
The turbo-generator at Lithuania's Ignalina atomic power station has a capacity of 1,450 megawatts.

Highest power line
A line 200 m (670 ft) high spans the Straits of Messina in Italy.

First battery
In 1800, Volta made a battery from a stack of copper and zinc plates.

Layers of brine-soaked cloth

Many copper and zinc plates increased the voltage of the battery

FIRST BATTERY, 1800

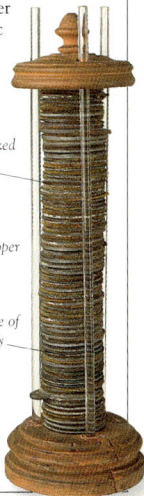

SCIENCE AND TECHNOLOGY

Widest bridge: Sydney Harbour bridge, Australia

INVENTIONS

FROM THE WHEEL to the light bulb and jet engine, inventions to make life easier have developed over the centuries. Some gadgets and ideas have been total failures; others have changed our world.

Clutch lever

BUDDING'S LAWN MOWER, 1830

Roller to flatten grass

Lawn mower was 48 cm (19 in) wide

DOMESTIC FIRSTS

First carpet
Floor coverings were first made with reeds. Chinese or Persian knotted carpets date from about 500 BC.

First mechanical clock
Mechanical clocks were first built in Europe about AD 1290.

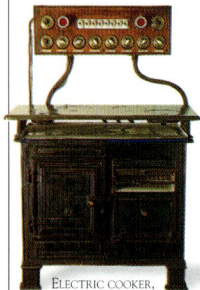

ELECTRIC COOKER, c.1900

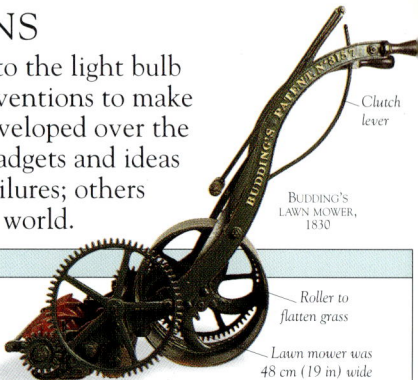

First lawn mower
Englishman Edwin Budding invented a lawn mower in 1830.

First light bulb
Joseph Swan, UK, and Thomas Edison, USA, are both credited with inventing the light bulb between 1878 and 1879.

First electric kettle
The US Carpenter Electric Company made the first kettle in 1891.

First electric oven
Also in 1891, the Carpenter Electric Company (above) sold the first electric oven.

First vacuum cleaner
Hubert Booth designed a horse-drawn electric vacuum cleaner in 1901.

First food mixer
US milkshake parlours used food mixers in the early 1900s. Multi-purpose mixers appeared in the 1930s.

First pop-up toaster
American breakfasts became much more exciting in the 1930s, with the pop-up toaster.

First nylon
Du Pont invented nylon in 1934. Toothbrushes were their first products.

ENGINE RECORDS

First steam-powered piston engine
In 1712, Newcomen, UK, built a steam-powered piston engine to pump water.

First internal combustion engine
In 1860, Etienne Lenoir designed an internal combustion engine.

JET ENGINE

First four-stroke car engine
In the 1880s, Germans Daimler and Benz developed the four-stroke engine, used in early motor cars.

First jet engine
Frank Whittle, UK, built the first jet engine prototype in 1937.

INVENTION RECORDS

First weighing scales
In 3500 BC, the first beam-balance scales appeared in ancient Egypt for weighing gold.

First wheel
The first wheels were used in Mesopotamia in about 3200 BC.

EARLY BOX OF MATCHES

First spinning wheel
Spinning wheels were used in India and China in the early 11th century AD to spin cotton yarn and silk.

First matches
Safety matches were introduced in Sweden in about 1850.

First electric lamp
The famous American inventor, Thomas Edison, produced the first working electric lamp in 1879.

First zip fastener
Whitcomb Judson, USA, invented the zip in 1891. His design was improved in 1914.

Highly resistant carbon filament

An air pump was used to create a partial vacuum, so the filament burnt less quickly

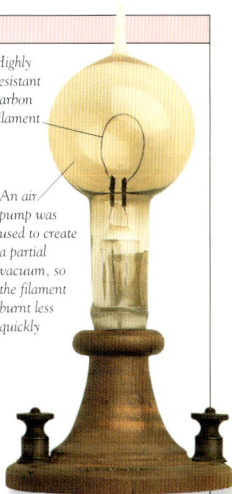

EDISON'S ELECTRIC LAMP

MEDICINE

EARLY PEOPLE thought that illnesses were
punishments from the gods. As doctors'
knowledge of the human body has grown
over the centuries, the causes
of many illnesses have been
identified and cures found.

ASPIRIN TINS,
c.1930

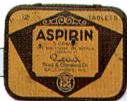

MEDICINE FIRSTS

First doctor
Hippocrates (c.460–377
BC) a Greek doctor, ran
a medical school on Kos
island. His guidelines
for doctors are still used.

First vaccination
In 1796, Edward Jenner,
UK, discovered a
vaccine for a very
common fatal
disease,
smallpox.

First anaesthetic
Laughing gas (nitrous
oxide) was used in 1844
by US dentist, Horace
Wells. W. Morton made
a more effective ether
inhaler in 1846.

First aspirin
Aspirin comes from the
bark of the white willow
tree. Synthetic aspirin
was first produced in
Germany in 1853.

First antiseptic
Carbolic acid was first
used as an antiseptic by
English surgeon, Joseph
Lister, in 1865. Before
this, germs were killers.

First antibiotics
Penicillin, the first
antibiotic drug, was
discovered by Scottish
doctor Alexander
Fleming in 1928. It
is now widely used to
treat once fatal diseases,
such as pneumonia.

First insulin
The use of the hormone,
insulin, as a treatment
for diabetes was
discovered in 1921.
Canadian scientists
extracted insulin from
the pancreas of pigs.

ANAESTHETIC
INHALER

Patient
inhales
vapour

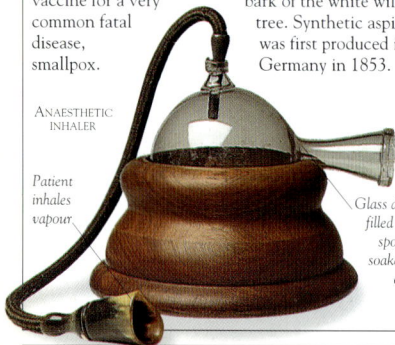

Glass dome
filled with
sponges
soaked in
ether

MEDICAL EQUIPMENT FIRSTS

Glass cylinder holds vaccine to be injected

SYRINGE, C.1865

First ambulance
The first ambulance, a light cart drawn by horses, was invented in 1792 by Baron Dominique-Jean Larrey, an army surgeon.

First stethoscope
In 1816, French doctor René Laënnec used a rolled paper to listen to a patient's chest.

First syringe
The first hypodermic syringe was devised in 1853 by Frenchman Charles Pravaz.

First X-rays
In 1895, German Röntgen named the mysterious rays from his vacuum tube "X-rays".

First pacemaker
A pacemaker, which artificially controls a heartbeat, was first fitted in 1954 in Sweden.

ARTIFICIAL HEART

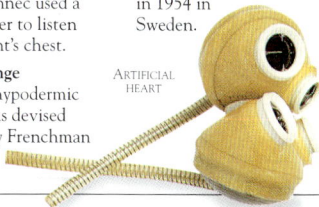

First endoscope
Fibre-optic endoscopes, for looking inside a patient's body, were developed in 1957 by US doctors Curtis, Hirschowitz, and Peters.

First CT scanner
CT (computerized tomography) scans take images of the brain and other soft tissue. They first appeared in 1972.

First artificial heart
The first artificial heart was fitted and pumped blood successfully for 16 weeks, in 1982.

PERSONAL HEALTH FIRSTS

First spectacles
Reading glasses were first made in Italy in about 1250. Glass-makers ground the lenses into shape.

First false teeth
Porcelain false teeth were invented in 1770.

First condom
The first condoms were linen. By 1800, they were made of sheep gut.

First contraceptive pill
Trials of the pill, which uses artificial hormones to prevent pregnancy, began in 1954.

PORCELAIN FALSE TEETH

De Chemant, France, devised false teeth with springs to hold them in place

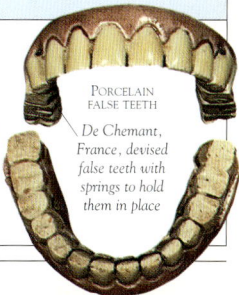

BUILDINGS

SINCE ANCIENT times, people have built ever taller and grander structures; buildings for living, working, shopping, and entertainment. Materials and construction methods are constantly being improved.

PETRONAS TOWERS, MALAYSIA

WORLD'S TALLEST BUILDINGS

Tallest free-standing tower
At 555 m (1,821 ft) high, the CN (Canadian National) Tower in Toronto is the world's tallest free-standing structure. It was built as a television transmitter in 1975.

Tallest artificial structure
The KTHI-TV mast in North Dakota, USA, stands a sky-scraping 629 m (2,064 ft) high, making it the world's tallest artificial structure. Built in 1963, the mast is supported by long, steel guy ropes.

Tallest block of flats
The 100-storey John Hancock tower in Chicago, USA, stands 343.5 m (1,127 ft) tall. Super-fast lifts can take passengers to the 94th floor in just 39 seconds. The building has 703 residential units.

Tallest hotel
When it is completed, the Ryuijyong Hotel in North Korea will be the world's tallest hotel, some 105 storeys high. It takes over from the Westin Stamford Hotel, Singapore.

TALLEST HABITABLE BUILDING
The twin Petronas Towers in Kuala Lumpur, Malaysia, stand 451.9 m (1,483 ft) high, with 88 storeys. A sky-bridge connects the towers half way up. At the base is a six-storey shopping centre.

FIRST ARCHITECT

The respected and worshipped Egyptian architect, Imhotep, designed and built the first pyramid for the Pharaoh Djoser, in about 2680 BC. It had stepped, rather than sloping sides.

Step pyramids like this were constructed in the Nile Valley between 2650 and 2150 BC

STEP PYRAMID

BUILDING RECORDS

Oldest building
In 1965, remains of a group of 400,000-year-old huts were found in Nice, France.

Biggest church
Ivory Coast's The Basilica of Our Lady of Peace at Yamoussoukro, seats 7,000 worshippers.

Biggest castle
The Czech Republic's Prague Castle was founded in AD 850.

Largest palace
The Palace of Versailles near Paris is 580 m (1,903 ft) long.

Biggest shopping centre
The West Edmonton Mall, Alberta, Canada contains 11 department stores and 800 shops.

Largest office building
About 50,000 people work in New York's World Trade Center, which has 1 million sq m (1 billion sq ft) of office space.

Largest restaurant
At the Royal Dragon restaurant in Bangkok, Thailand, 541 waiters deliver dishes to 5,000 diners on roller skates to ensure a speedy service.

Largest sports stadium
The Strahov Stadium in Prague, Czech Republic, seats 240,000 spectators. It was built in 1934.

Open stadium was built for displays involving 40,000 gymnasts

STRAHOV STADIUM, PRAGUE

BRIDGES, TUNNELS, CANALS, AND DAMS

FROM TRAFFIC-LADEN bridges and tunnels, to canals and tall dams, record-breaking feats of engineering are found all over the world.

SUSPENSION BRIDGE

ARCH BRIDGE

CANTILEVER BRIDGE

CABLE-STAYED BRIDGE

BASCULE BRIDGE

BEAM BRIDGE

BRIDGE RECORDS

First iron bridge
In 1779, the first iron bridge was built in Shropshire, UK. Before this bridges were made of wood or stone.

Longest bridge
Crossing Lake Pontchartrain in the USA, the world's longest bridge is almost 39 km (24 miles) long.

Longest suspension bridge span
The Japanese Akashi Kaikyo bridge spans 1,990 m (6,529 ft).

Longest cable-stayed bridge
Pont de Normandie, France, has a main span of 856 m (2,808 ft).

Highest bridge
The Royal Gorge suspension bridge, Arkansas River, Colorado, USA, is 321 m (1,053 ft) above sea level.

Widest long-span bridge
Australia's Sydney Harbour Bridge is 49 m (160 ft) wide. It has eight traffic lanes, cycle paths, and railway tracks.

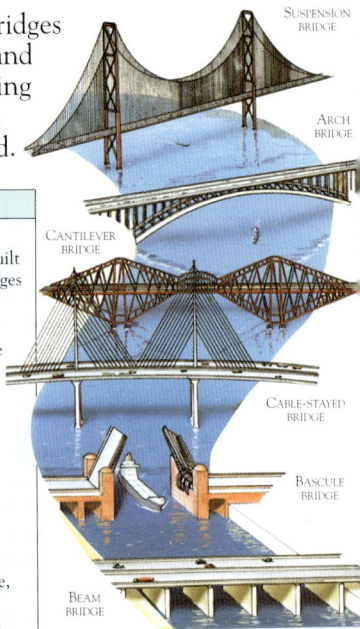

BRIDGE TYPES

There are many types of bridge, suited for different terrain. Most rest on sturdy supports, often steel or concrete beams and cables, fixed securely to the ground.

WORLD'S LONGEST TUNNELS

Longest road tunnel
The St Gotthard Road Tunnel in Switzerland is an amazing feat of engineering that has allowed travel through the Alps. It stretches for 16 km (10 miles).

Longest water tunnel
At 169 km (105 miles) long, the West Delaware tunnel supplies water to New York City and is the longest tunnel of all.

Longest undersea tunnel
Linking England and France, the Channel Tunnel is 50 km (31 miles) long.

Longest rail tunnel
The 54-km (33½-mile) Seikan Rail Tunnel links the islands of Honshu and Hokkaido.

SEIKAN RAIL TUNNEL, JAPAN

CANAL RECORDS

Oldest canal
Built in Sumer (now Iraq) around 4000 BC, the oldest canals were only discovered in 1968.

Busiest canal
Each year, some 43,000 ships pass through the Kiel Canal in Germany.

Longest canal
Opened in 1869, the Suez Canal, which links the Mediterranean and Red Seas, has a length of 174 km (108 miles).

Most canals
The Netherlands has a record 8,000 km (4,971 miles) of canals.

Largest lock
The Berendrecht lock in Antwerp, Belgium, is 500 m (1,640 ft) long and 68 m (223 ft) wide.

SUEZ CANAL

DAM RECORDS

Oldest known dam
The Egyptian Sadd el-Kafara dam was built as long ago as 5,000 years. The main construction materials were simply rocks and earth.

Largest dam
The Syncrude Tailings dam in Canada has a massive volume of 540 million cu m (706 million cu ft).

Tallest dam
Tajikistan's Rogunsky Dam is an enbankment that measures 325 m (1,066 ft) in height.

SHIPS AND BOATS

THE FIRST BOATS were simple canoes, hollowed out of tree trunks about 9,000 years ago. Today, giant liners, merchant ships, and oil tankers sail the seas, carrying passengers and goods all over the world.

Square sails catch the wind, propelling the boat forward

VESSEL RECORDS

Oldest sailing boat
The first boats with sails were probably made by the ancient Egyptians in around 3100 BC.

Largest yacht
Built in 1984, the *Abdul Aziz* is 147 m (482 ft) in length. It is owned by the Saudi Arabian royal family.

Largest passenger liner
The Norway, built in 1961, accommodates 2,022 passengers and 900 crew.

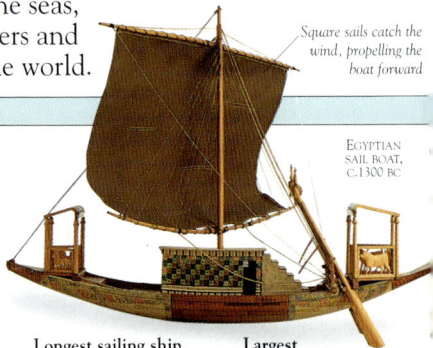

EGYPTIAN SAIL BOAT, C.1300 BC

SHIN AITOKU MARU

Computer-controlled sails are opened according to the wind

Longest sailing ship
The 187-m (613-ft) long *Club Med 1* cruises around the islands of the Caribbean. It was built in France.

Largest sailing ship
As long as 4½ tennis courts, the *France II* measured 127.7 m (418 ft) in length.

First computer sails
In 1980, the Japanese *Shin Aitoku Maru* was fitted with computer-controlled sails.

Unluckiest ship
In 1912, the *Titanic* struck an iceberg, losing 1,500 lives.

SHIPPING RECORDS

Largest container ship
Denmark's *Regina Maersk* can carry 6,000 standard-size containers, each 6 m (20 ft) long.

First oil tanker
Wellfield, launched in 1924, was one of the world's first large oil tankers. Her cargo of crude oil was stored in her hull.

Largest ship
It takes five minutes to walk end to end on the *Jahre Viking*, a 458-m (1,503-ft) long Norwegian oil tanker.

Largest merchant fleet
Panama's massive merchant fleet can carry goods weighing up to 72 million tonnes (70 million tons).

Top ship builders
South Korea has a booming economy. About 20 per cent of the world's ships are made in this country.

World's busiest port
Rotterdam, in the Netherlands, handles more than 287 million tonnes (283 million tons) of goods every day.

OIL TANKER
WELLFIELD

Oil was poured into compartments

Wellfield weighed 6,000 tonnes (5,905 tons)

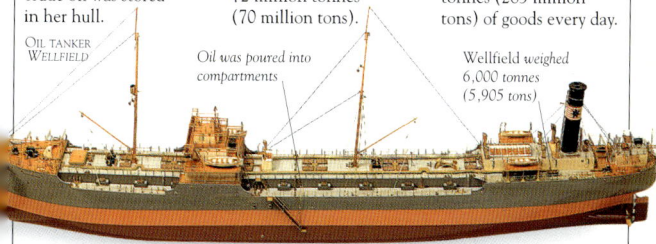

SUBMARINE RECORDS

First built submarine
A wooden submarine appeared in the 1620s. It had to be rowed along underwater!

Fastest submarines
Russian Alfa-class nuclear submarines can speed through water at 83 km/h (52 mph).

OTHER WATER RECORDS

First Atlantic crossing
In 1819, the American boat *Savannah* became the first to steam across the Atlantic Ocean.

First lifeboat
Sturdy, rowing lifeboats were launched in Europe in the 1800s, designed to save lives.

First hovercraft
In the 1950s, Christopher Cockerell, UK, invented the hovercraft, which floats on a cushion of air.

Largest hovercraft
Built in 1968, the SR-N4 hovercraft speeds at 120 km/h (75 mph).

TRAINS

THE FIRST railways were built more than 150 years ago. Today, the world's railway tracks would circle the Earth more than a hundred times, if they were laid end to end.

FIRST LOCOMOTIVE Stephenson's "Rocket", built in 1829, is one of the most famous steam engines.

TRAIN RECORDS

First steam locomotive
In 1804, Trevithick built a steam locomotive for pulling wagons in Wales.

First public railway
In 1830, a service opened in the UK, between Liverpool and Manchester, for carrying goods and passengers.

Most luxurious train
South Africa's Cape Town–Pretoria *Blue Train* is hailed as "a five-star hotel on wheels".

Longest train journey
Russia's Trans-Siberian line travels 9,297 km (5,777 miles) from Moscow to Vladivostok continuously.

Fastest train
The French TGV (*Train à Grande Vitesse*) made a record trip at 515 km/h (320 mph) in May 1990.

Most powerful steam locomotive
In 1938, the *Mallard* set a world speed record for a steam locomotive of 203 km/h (126 mph).

MALLARD
STEAM LOCOMOTIVE

R 4468

STATIONS RECORDS

Oldest station
Liverpool Road Station in Manchester, UK, was first used in 1830 but closed in 1975.

Largest station
The bustling Grand Central Terminal, New York, USA, has no fewer than 44 platforms.

Highest station
Condor station, in Bolivia, stands as high as 4,786 m (15,705 ft) above sea level.

Longest platform
At State Street Center Subway in Chicago, USA, the platform is 1,067 m (3,500 ft) long.

MORE TRAIN RECORDS

First driverless train
A train line operated by computer opened in Lille, France in 1983.

First monorail
Opened in 1901, the German Wuppertal still makes its 13-km (8-mile) trip above the River Wupper.

EARLY ELECTRIC LOCOMOTIVE, 1904

Current is collected from overhead power line

NORTH EASTERN

Most powerful diesel
The *Deltic* diesel train, built in 1956, was the most powerful diesel-electric in its time.

First electric railway
Signalling the end of the steam age, the first public electric trains ran in Germany in 1881.

First underground train
Connecting Paddington to Farringdon Street in London, UK, the first underground railway in the world opened in 1863. It ran on steam.

Longest tube network
London's underground, UK, contains 393 km (244 miles) of track.

DELTIC DIESEL ELECTRIC LOCOMOTIVE

CARS

THE FIRST mass-produced cars appeared less than a hundred years ago. Since then, cars have changed our world. By the year 2025, the roads may carry a billion vehicles.

Top speed was 13 km/h (8 mph)

FIRST MOTOR CAR
The "Motorwagen", a petrol-driven three-wheeler, was built by the German engineer Karl Benz, in 1886.

MOTOR CAR RECORDS

First production line
In 1910, the Model T Ford was the first car to come off a production line. By 1924, the US Ford Motor Company had manufactured ten million cars.

Top car manufacturer
With nine million cars rolling off its production lines ever year, Japan is the world's top car-producing country. Cars are the country's leading export.

Longest car
At 30.5 m (100 ft) long, the world's longest car is a 26-wheeled limousine from the USA. Inside, it has a swimming pool and king-sized bed, and it bends in the middle to go round corners!

All Model T's had black paintwork

Seats lined with wood and finished with leather

A 2,898 cc engine enabled top speed of 65 km/h (40 mph)

MODEL T FORD, 1914

SPEED RECORDS

Fastest non-racing car
The *Jaguar XJ220* has a maximum speed of 349 km/h (217 mph). Hot on its tail is the Lamborghini Diablo, racing along at 325 km/h (202 mph).

Fastest diesel car
The *Mercedes C111/3* reached 327 km/h (203 mph) in Italian tests during the 1970's. It also covered a record 3,774 km (2,345 miles) in 12 hours.

Bonnet space for luggage as engine is in boot

"Soft-top" folding roof

VOLKSWAGEN BEETLE

BEST-SELLING CAR
Since production began in Germany in 1937, about 21,220,000 Volkswagen *Beetles* have been sold worldwide, making them the best-selling car ever.

Smallest car
Measuring only 1.34 m (4⅜ ft) in length, the *Peel* is one of the smallest cars ever built. It has no reverse gear.

First front-wheel drive
The UK's Austin *Mini-cooper* was the first front-wheel drive car to have its engine and gearbox fitted parallel to the axle.

Highest price for a car
The record-breaking sum of $15 million was paid for a 1962 *Ferrari 250 GTO* in 1989.

Most people in a mini
The popular Austin *Mini* was first produced in 1958. Since then, people have attempted to squeeze many people inside one. The record currently stands at 24.

AUSTIN MINI COOPER S, 1963

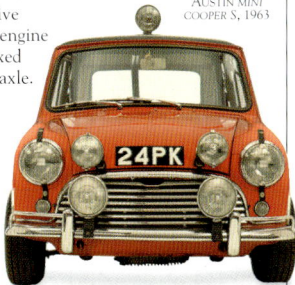

24PK

GREEN CAR RECORDS

Streamlined design enables *Genius E* to travel faster

Lowest petrol consumption
The economical *Genius E*, produced by Japan's Honda, uses petrol at a rate of 2,279 km/l (6,409 mpg).

Fastest solar power car
In 1988, General Motors' solar-powered *Sunraycer* reached 78.4 km/h (48.71 mph) on sunlight alone. Its special panels convert the sunlight into electrical energy.

ROAD TRANSPORT

THE FIRST MAJOR roads were built by the Romans some 2,000 years ago so their armies could cross their vast empire. Today, most countries have busy road networks, linking villages, towns, and cities.

FIRST TYRES
Vehicles were first fitted with solid rubber tyres, replaced by peumatic (air-filled) tyres from 1895.

ROAD RECORDS

Busiest road
At the peak of the rush hour, 25,500 vehicles crawl along a 1.5-km (1-mile) stretch of Interstate 405 in California, USA.

Longest road
The Pan-American Highway runs 24,140 km (15,000 miles) through the USA to Brazil.

Highest road
In places, the road between Tibet and Xinjiang in China lies 5,633 m (18,480 ft) above sea level.

Widest road
The six-lane Monumental Axis in Brasilia, Brazil measures an amazing 250 m (820 ft) – the widest road in the world!

First motorway
In 1921, an autobahn (motorway) opened in Berlin, Germany.

FIRST AUTOBAHN, GERMANY

Room for two passengers

Driver sat at the front, exposed to the weather

Solid wheels made journey uncomfortable

FIRST METERED TAXICAB
Arguments between taxi drivers and passengers over fares were all too common, so the first metered cabs took to Germany's roads in 1896. The idea spread quickly.

BERSEY ELECTRIC TAXI, 1897

PUBLIC TRANSPORT RECORDS

First electric tram
The first electric trams ran in London, UK, in 1901, replacing horse-pulled trams and providing fast transport for city dwellers.

First double decker
Double decker buses were first seen on the streets of London, UK in 1919. Travellers on the top deck were open to the elements!

First motor coach
Motor coaches first appeared in 1926 in the UK. They allowed people who did not own their own cars to enjoy a ride in the country.

ELECTRIC TRAM, 1901

Largest bus fleet
More than 11,000 buses carry passengers around São Paulo, Brazil.

Longest bus route
A bus travels 9,660 km (6,003 miles) from Venezuela to Argentina.

Largest tram system
St Petersburg, Russia, has some 2,400 tram cars running 64 routes.

Largest taxi fleet
There is no shortage of taxis in Mexico City – it has 60,000 of them!

OTHER VEHICLE RECORDS

Fastest rocket-powered
The *Budweiser Rocket* car reached a speed of 1,190 km/h (739 mph).

Land speed record
The jet-powered *Thrust SSC* broke the sound barrier in the Nevada desert, USA, in 1997, with an average speed of 1,228 km/h (763 mph).

Largest land vehicle
Two gigantic crawlers, used to take space shuttles to their launch pads at Cape Canaveral, USA, weigh 8,000 tonnes (7,874 tons).

Sidewinder missile for extra speed

BUDWEISER ROCKET CAR

Stan Barrett reached just under the speed of sound

BICYCLES AND MOTORBIKES

THERE ARE at least 800 million bicycles in the world today, outnumbering cars by two to one. The motorized bicycle, or motorbike, first appeared in Germany in 1885.

No pedals or brakes

FIRST BICYCLE
Built in 1817, this early German bicycle was called a "running machine" or "hobby horse".

BICYCLE RECORDS

VELOCIPEDE, 1869

First bike with pedals
The first bicycle, the velocipede, was invented by a Scottish blacksmith, Kirkpatrick Macmillan, in 1839.

First tandem
The first successful tandem bicycles (for two riders) were made in Britain in 1886.

First mountain bike
The first all-terrain mountain bike was built in 1989 by Americans Charles Kelly and Gary Fisher.

Sturdy, lightweight frame and thick tyres

Longest bicycle
In 1988, a 22.24-m (73-ft) long bicycle was built. Four riders took it 246 m (807 ft).

Most bicycles
In China there are 300 million bicycles.

Fastest cyclist
In 1985, John Howard, USA, reached 245.08 km/h (152.3 mph) on his specially designed bicycle.

MOUNTAIN BIKE, 1989

MOTORBIKE RECORDS

First motorbike
In 1885, Daimler, a German engineer, fitted an internal combustion engine to a wooden bicycle.

Fastest motorcyclist
In 1990, US rider Dave Campos reached more than 500 km/h (311 mph).

First "superbike"
Produced in 1968 by Honda of Japan, the first "superbike" (large, powerful motorbike) had a four-cylinder engine.

Motorbike compared to an egg

SMALLEST MOTORBIKE

Smallest motorbike
Shown above, this tiny motorbike had a front wheel diameter of 1.9 cm (¾ in) and was ridden for 1 m (3 ft 4 in).

Longest motorbike
Designed and built by an American, Gregg Reid, the longest street-legal motorbike stretched for 4.57 m (15 ft).

Top speed of 190 km/h (120 mph)

Instruments

Disc brakes

HONDA CB750, 1967

STUNT RECORDS

Longest ramp jump
Doug Danger of the USA jumped 76.5 m (251 ft) on a 991 Honda CR 500.

Longest wheelie
In 1991, Yauyuki Kudo of Japan rode a wheelie (riding non-stop on the back wheel) for 331 km (205¼ miles).

Fastest wheelie
Belgian Jacky Vranken achieved a wheelie at 254.07 km/h (157.87 mph) in 1992.

Largest pyramid
In 1995, the Indian Army motorcycle display team created a pyramid of 133 men on 11 motorbikes.

MOST ON A MOTORBIKE
In 1995, in Brasília, Brazil, 47 people managed to ride on a single motorbike for 1.6 km (1 mile).

AIRCRAFT

SINCE THE FIRST POWERED FLIGHT in 1903, aircraft have developed rapidly. Today, air transport has opened up the world, allowing people to travel faster and further than before.

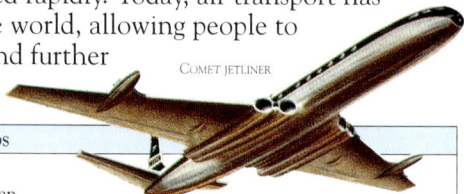

COMET JETLINER

AEROPLANE RECORDS

First flight
In 1903, the American Wright brothers first flew their petrol-driven *Wright Flyer* biplane.

First transatlantic flight
British aviators Alcock and Brown made the 16-hour trip in 1919.

First jetliner
The De Havilland *Comet* jetliner first came into service in 1952.

Fastest jet plane
US Air Force spy plane, *Blackbird*, reached a speed of 3,530 km/h (2,193 mph) in 1976.

Fastest passenger plane
Supersonic *Concorde* flies New York – London in three hours, twice as fast as ordinary planes.

Largest airliner
The Boeing 747-400 has seats for 567 people.

Widest wingspan
Hughes H4 Hercules flying boat, *Spruce Goose*, had a wingspan of 97.51 m (320 ft).

Heaviest plane
Russia's *Dream* can take-off weighing up to 600 tonnes (590 tons).

Worst air disaster
In 1977, two Boeings collided in Tenerife, killing 583 people.

CONCORDE

AIRPORT RECORDS

First modern airport
Gatwick airport was built in 1928 near London, UK.

Largest airport
The King Khalid airport outside Riyadh, Saudi Arabia, opened in 1983.

Busiest airport
Each year, Chicago's O'Hare airport, USA, handles 900,000 planes.

HELICOPTER RECORDS

First helicopter
The first practical helicopter, the *Focke Achgelis FW-61*, was flown in 1936.

Fastest helicopter
In 1986, a Westland Lynx helicopter flew at an average speed of 400 km/h (249 mph).

Largest helicopter
A Russian Mil Mi-12 helicopter weighed 103 tonnes (101 tons).

AIRSHIP RECORDS

First airship
In 1852, Frenchman Henri Giffard built and flew a steam airship.

First around the world
In 1929, Germany's *Graf Zeppelin* completed the trip in 21 days, 5 hours, and 31 minutes.

First passenger airship
Germany's *Hindenburg* was the first to fly people to the USA.

Largest airship
At 245 m (804 ft) long, the *Hindenburg* first flew in 1936, cruising at 126 km/h (78 mph).

GRAF ZEPPELIN

MORE AIRCRAFT RECORDS

First balloon flight
Father Bartolomeu de Gusmao invented a hot-air balloon that was flown in Portugal in 1709.

Largest hot-air balloon
Richard Branson's *Virgin Otsuka Pacific Flyer*, of 1991, held 73,624 cu m (2,600,000 cu ft) of heated air.

Furthest flown in a hot-air balloon
In 1995, Steve Fossett flew a hot-air balloon 8,748 km (5,435 miles) across the Pacific Ocean.

Strong frame

Engine

Streamlined fibreglass seat to carry pilot

MICROLIGHT, 1990

First microlight aircraft
The first microlights were flown in 1990, in the UK. Their wings spanned 10.3 m (34 ft). Before microlights, propellers and engines were fitted to gliders.

SPACE EXPLORATION

THE SPACE AGE began in 1957, with the launch of the first satellite. Rapid technological advances since then have enabled people to walk on the Moon and take photographs of Mars.

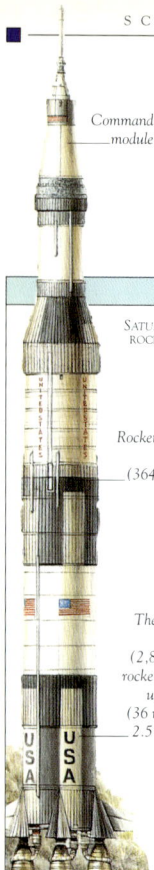

Command module

SATURN V ROCKET

Rocket stands 111 m (364 ft) tall

The 2,902-tonne (2,856-ton) rocket is lifted up 58 km (36 miles) in 2.5 minutes

SPACECRAFT RECORDS

First to the Moon
The first mission to land successfully on the Moon was the USA's *Apollo 11* in 1969.

Last Moon mission
In 1972, *Apollo 17* became the last manned mission to the Moon.

First planetary probe
In 1970, the former USSR's *Venera 7* landed on Venus.

Furthest probe
In 1986, *Pioneer 10* became the first probe to leave the Solar System when it crossed Pluto's orbit.

Most powerful engine
The F1 engine of the *Saturn V* rocket, used for Apollo Moon missions, is the most powerful.

First re-usable shuttle
Columbia is a self-sufficient space shuttle that flies home like a plane. Before this, only the command module would return to Earth, leaving the rocket floating in space.

SPACE SHUTTLE COLUMBIA

Fuel tank

Rocket booster

Space shuttle orbiter

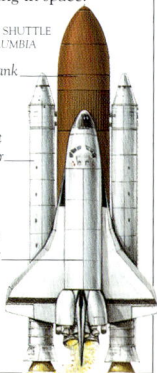

ASTRONAUT RECORDS

First man in space
In 1961, Russian cosmonaut, Yuri Gagarin flew into space in *Vostok I*.

First woman in space
In 1963, Valentina Tereshkova, entered space in *Vostok 6*.

MANNED MANOEUVRING UNIT

Astronauts can space walk without being tied to shuttle

First "jetpack"
Manned manoeuvring units, or "jetpacks" were invented in 1984.

Longest in space
Musa Manarov spent 365 days, 39 minutes, and 47 seconds on *Mir*.

First person on Moon
In 1969, Neil Armstrong of *Apollo 11* walked on the Moon.

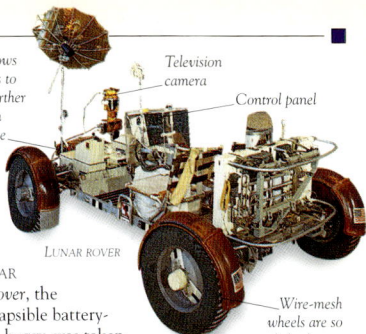

Buggy allows astronauts to explore further afield than landing site

Television camera

Control panel

LUNAR ROVER

SPACE CAR
Lunar Rover, the first collapsible battery-powered buggy, was taken on the *Apollo 15* Moon mission in 1971.

Wire-mesh wheels are so light that on Earth they would be crushed by the car's weight

ASTRONOMY RECORDS

First to observe space with telescope
In 1609, Galileo Galilei first used a telescope to look into space.

Biggest telescope
Set on Hawaii's Mauna Kea, the *Keck 1* has a 10-m (33-ft) mirror.

Longest space telescope
Launched in 1990, the *Hubble* space telescope weighs 11 tonnes (10½ tons) and is 13 m (43 ft) long.

Largest radio telescope
Puerto Rico's *Arecibo* telescope dish is 305 m (1,000 ft) wide.

Oldest observatory
The oldest surviving astronomical observatory was built in South Korea in AD 632.

Highest observatory
An observatory on Mt Chacaltaya, Bolivia, sits 5,200 m (17,060 ft) above sea level.

Antenna transmits images to Earth

HUBBLE SPACE TELESCOPE

COMMUNICATIONS

FROM THE FIRST post box to sending messages via the Internet, advances in communications have revolutionized our lives. Today, the telephone and fax allow us to make global contact in an instant.

FIRST POSTBOX

WORLD MAIL RECORDS

First stamp
Prepaid, sticky postage stamps – the penny black and two-penny blue – were first issued in 1840, in the UK.

First postbox
A postbox was put up in 1852 in Guernsey, Channel Islands.

First postcard
Postcards were first sent in 1861 and were all the rage by 1870.

PENNY BLACK STAMP, 1840

The stamp had a sticky gummed back not unlike today's

First air mail
Air mail began in 1919, in the UK and France.

First automatic sorting
Electronic mail sorting was introduced in the USA in the 1960s, speeding up the process by up to ten times.

Most post handled
The US Postal Service annually handles 170 billion letters.

Biggest e-mail user
In the USA, 4,000 million electronic mail messages are sent yearly.

FIRST POSTCARDS, 1861

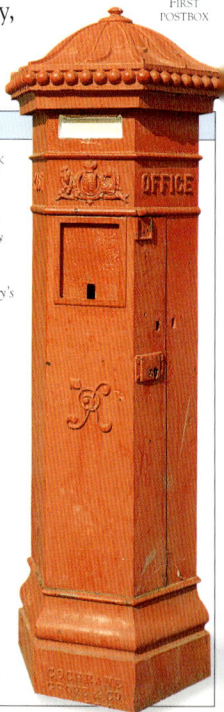

TELEPHONE AND FAX RECORDS

TWO BELL TELEPHONES, 1876

First telephone call
Alexander Graham Bell sent the first telephone message in 1876.

First dial telephone
US undertaker Almon Strowger invented dial telephones in 1889 when he found that operators had been taking bribes to divert his calls to competitors.

First mobile phone
The mobile phone idea came from the USA in the 1940s, but it took 30 years to implement.

First videophone
British Telecom, UK is amongst those developing practical video screen telephones.

Most mobile phones
Per head, Sweden has the most subscribers, with 229 mobile phones for every 1,000 people.

Smallest fax machine
Held in your hand, the smallest fax machine weighs just 140 g (5 oz).

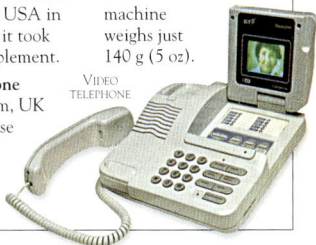

VIDEO TELEPHONE

COMPUTER RECORDS

First personal computer
1977 saw the first personal computer, *Commodore PET*.

First floppy disc
Floppy discs were first produced in 1970 by US company IBM.

Fastest computer
The CM-5 at Los Alamos National Laboratories, USA, performs 131 billion operations a second.

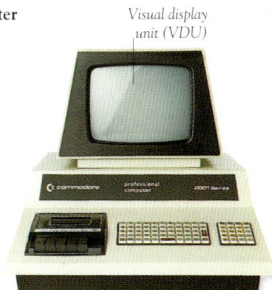

Visual display unit (VDU)

COMMODORE PERSONAL COMPUTER

Largest computer firm
IBM, USA, employs about 220,000 people.

Largest software firm
Microsoft, USA, the leading software producer, employs 16,140 people.

Largest network
Since the launch of the Internet in 1984, at least ten million computers have lined up to it.

ARTS AND THE MEDIA

Longest painting in production: Sistine Chapel

MUSICAL INSTRUMENTS

THE FIRST INSTRUMENTS were simple flutes
and whistles made from animal bones.
Today's instruments fall into five
families: keyboard, percussion,
brass, string, and woodwind.

GUITAR RECORDS

First acoustic guitar
The design of the
classical guitar
originates from mid-
19th-century Spain.

SPANISH
GUITAR

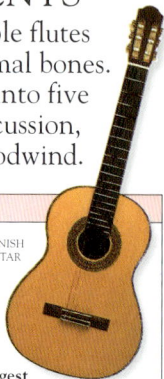

First electric guitar
The electric Fender
Stratocaster, or Strat,
was first played in 1954
and has changed very
little since then.

Largest
The biggest guitar is
11.63 m (38 ft) long,
4.9 m (16 ft) wide, and
weighs 446 kg (983 lb).

BOWED STRING INSTRUMENT RECORDS

Oldest
The earliest
bowed fiddles
date back to
AD 10.

First violins
Replacing
viols, violins
appeared in
Italy in 1550.

Smallest
The violin is the
smallest and highest
pitched instrument.

Largest and deepest
The double bass is
the largest and deepest
stringed instrument,
measuring 2 m (6½ ft)
from spike to scroll.

BRASS AND WIND INSTRUMENT RECORDS

First trumpet
The first trumpets date back to Roman times. Trumpets were as long as 1.5 m (5 ft) and were made in sections so they could be taken apart when not in use.

Largest brass instrument
Tubas can be 2.4 m (7¾ ft) tall. Uncoiled, the pipes would stretch 14 m (46 ft) in length.

First organ
Invented in Greece in 250 BC, the world's first organ blew air through its pipes by using water power.

Loudest wind instrument
The huge Auditorium Organ in Atlantic City, New Jersey, USA, makes as much noise as 25 brass bands.

TUBA

MORE INSTRUMENT RECORDS

First symphony orchestra
Founded in 1743, in Germany, the first symphony orchestra performed at the court of Duke Karl Theodor.

Largest orchestra
In June 1872, Johann Strauss the younger conducted an orchestra of 987 instruments in Boston, USA.

First piano
Italian instrument maker, Bartolomeo Cristofori, built the first piano in 1709.

First synthesizer
Master of artificial sound, the synthesizer appeared in the 1940s.

Favourite instrument
Millions of harmonicas are sold every year.

Most strings
Harps have up to 47 strings – more than any other stringed instrument.

Soundbox
IRISH HARP

PERCUSSION RECORDS

Largest drum
In 1987, a drum 3.96 m (13 ft) wide was played at London's Royal Festival Hall.

Biggest drum kit
A 112-piece drum kit including 88 drums, 18 cymbals, and 4 hi-hats, was constructed in New York, USA, in 1990.

Spookiest drum
Francis Drake's drum rolls by itself when England faces danger.

MUSIC

FROM A SIMPLE drum rhythm, to the sound of an orchestra or the latest chart-topping single, there are hundreds of musical styles. The ability to bring music into the home has introduced many musical genres to diverse audiences throughout the world.

Horn channels sound outward

MUSIC FIRSTS

Handle used to spin turntable

Steel needle rests on turntable

BERLINER'S RECORD PLAYER

First record player
German-born American, Emile Berliner, devised the first working record player in 1888. It was based on Thomas Edison's earlier phonograph.

First records
Records were cylindrical and made of wax until 1887, which saw the first flat, plastic records.

First cassette tape recorder
The Dutch electronics company Phillips was first to invent a tape recorder for playing cassettes. It was patented in 1963.

First study of music
The famous Greek thinker Pythagoras (c. 580–500 BC) was a leading intellectual of his time. He used a lyre, a stringed instrument, to make the first known study of music.

First printed music
Following the invention of the printing press by Johannes Gutenberg in 1440–1450, the first printed music appeared in Europe around 1480. This enabled a variety of pieces to be played.

CLASSICAL RECORDS

Longest opera
Die Meistersinger von Nurnberg lasts 5 hours.

Shortest opera
Rees and Reynolds' *The Sands of Time* is a short 4-minute opera.

Longest symphony
Rogers composed the 13-hour *Victory at Sea*.

SONY
WALKMAN

First personal stereo
In 1979, the Japanese company Sony made a portable stereo, or "Walkman" that did not need mains power.

First CDs
Plastic compact discs, or CDs, appeared in 1982. They hold coded music.

COMPACT
DISC

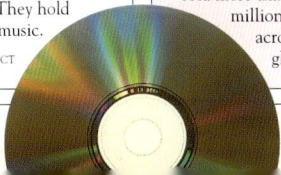

COMPOSER RECORDS

Youngest
Wolfgang Amadeus Mozart (1756–1791) was writing and playing music by the age of four and went on to be a great composer.

Fastest
Franz Schubert wrote some 1,000 works in just 18 years and five months. He died in 1828, aged just 35 years.

Most prolific
Austrian classical composer Joseph Haydn (1732–1809) wrote a total of 340 hours of music in his lifetime.

YOUNG MOZART

Most dextrous
Sergei Rachmaninov (1873–1943) could span 12 white piano keys with one hand.

Biggest musical family
The Bach family included 76 musicians, of whom Johann was the most talented.

WORLD POP MUSIC RECORDS

Biggest-selling single
Elton John's tribute to Princess Diana, *Candle in the Wind 1997*, sold 31.7 million copies in just 37 days.

Biggest-selling album
Thriller, produced by Michael Jackson has sold more than 45 million copies across the globe.

Most successful group
The Beatles are known throughout the world and sales have been estimated at more than one billion copies.

Most successful songwriter
Former Beatle Paul McCartney (b. 1942) has had 32 number one singles in the USA and 28 in the UK.

VISUAL ARTS

EVERY SOCIETY has its own works of art – paintings, sculptures, carvings, or photographs that capture an artist's personal vision and view of the world. Over the years, some artistic styles have changed little; others have moved on.

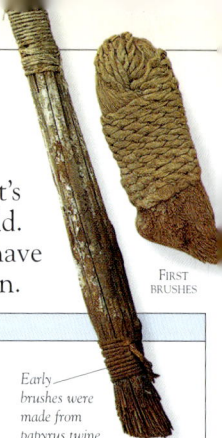

FIRST BRUSHES

PAINTING RECORDS

COLLAPSIBLE TIN PAINT TUBES, 19TH CENTURY

Lapis lazuli is ground up and put in tubes as ultramarine

LAPIS LAZULI

First paint
Paint was first made from ground stones such as lapis lazuli and kept in pigs' bladders. The first paint tubes appeared in the 19th century.

First paintbrushes
More than 4,000 years ago, Egyptians used thick rope paintbrushes.

Oldest paintings
France's Lascaux Caves are full of 17,000-year-old pictures of animals.

Most valuable painting
Leonardo da Vinci's (1452–1519) most famous painting *Mona Lisa* (below) was once assessed at $100 million for insurance purposes – far too costly to insure.

MONA LISA, 1503–1507

Early brushes were made from papyrus twine

Largest painting
In April 1995, US students made a 7,127.8 sq m (76,723 sq ft) painting of Elvis Presley.

Most stolen painting
Mona Lisa (see left) is recorded as the painting most often stolen and is among those most frequently reproduced.

Longest to paint
It took Michelangelo (1573–1610) four and a half years to paint the ceiling of Rome's Sistine Chapel. The painting covers more than 900 sq m (9,687 sq ft).

ARTIST RECORDS

Most versatile
Not only was the Italian Leonardo da Vinci (1452–1519) a master painter, he was also a sculptor, architect, engineer, musician, biologist, and scientist.

Longest forgotten
The works of Italian artist, Sandro Botticelli (1445–1510) lay forgotten from his death in 1510 until the 19th century.

Most prolific artist
In his lifetime, Pablo Picasso (1881–1973) produced at least 13,500 paintings, 100,000 prints, 34,000 book illustrations, and about 300 sculptures.

Best forger
From 1937 to 1943, Dutch artist, Hans van Meergeren, managed to paint and sell six forged Vermeers and two fake Pieter de Hoochs.

PHOTOGRAPHY RECORDS

First photo
The earliest photograph was produced in 1827 by Frenchman Niepce.

First colour photo
Scottish James Maxwell colour-photographed a tartan ribbon in 1861.

First 35mm camera
A 35mm camera appeared in 1914, but the Leica was the first to be taken seriously.

Most valuable photo
A photograph of the hands of US painter, Georgia O'Keeffe was sold in New York, in 1993 for £398,500.

Leica was the first to use 36 exposures

35MM LEICA CAMERA, 1924

SCULPTURE RECORDS

"VENUS" FIGURINE, FRANCE, C. 27,000 BC

Pregnant woman may signify mother goddess

First sculpture
Clay statues of pregnant women found in France were made in about 27,000 BC.

Tallest statue
The statue of Chief Crazy Horse on Thunderhead Mountain, USA, is 195 m (640 ft) tall.

Largest sculpture
The figures of General Robert Lee, Jefferson Davis, and General Thomas Jackson carved into Stone Mountain, USA, are 27.4 m (90 ft) high.

THE WRITTEN WORD

INVENTED IN SUMER (Iraq) some 5,500 years ago for accounting and recording historical details, writing has become one of our most important means of information and communication.

EGYPTIAN REED PENS

WRITING FIRSTS

First typewriter
Produced by US Remington Company, the first typewriter appeared in 1874.

STANDARD TYPEWRITER

First writing
The Sumerians were the first to write down their language, using wedge-shaped symbols (called cuneiform) for words.

First alphabet
The first true alphabet, in which individual letters could be joined together to make words, appeared in Syria around 1300 BC.

First paper
Paper, made from the pulp of fibres of the mulberry tree, was invented in China in AD 105.

First pen
Ancient Egyptians wrote with pens made from lengths of reeds sharpened at the end.

FIRST PRINTING PRESS
Printing with movable type was a Chinese invention, but it took nearly 400 years to reach Europe. In the mid-15th century, a German goldsmith, Johannes Gutenberg, devised the first hand printing press using a screw mechanism similar to that used in wine-making.

Paper is attached to tympan, which folds over press stone

Platen presses down to make an impression of type on paper

Inked type set on press stone, which is wound under platen

HAND PRINTING PRESS

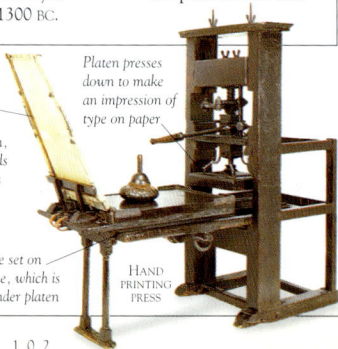

WRITER RECORDS

Best children's authors
Goscinny and Uderzo created the character of Astérix in 1959. Their 30 books sold 250,000 copies worldwide.

Oldest written poem
The Sumerian epic poem, *Gilgamesh*, was written in 2,000 BC.

First to use false name
Charlotte Brontë used the name Currer Bell for her novel *Jane Eyre*.

Most published author
William Shakespeare (1564–1616), the English playwright, is the most published author of all time.

WILLIAM SHAKESPEARE

BOOK RECORDS

Oldest book
Johannes Gutenberg printed 160 copies of the hand-decorated Gutenberg Bible on his press in 1455. He modelled it on early manuscript bibles. It was the first printed bible.

GUTENBERG BIBLE

First novel
The Tale of Genji, based on court life in Japan, was written in AD 1007 by Murasaki Shikibu.

First braille book
A Summary of French History, Century by Century, printed in 1837, was the first book for the blind.

Best-selling book
Estimates say six billion copies of the Bible have been sold since 1816, but no-one can be sure.

Largest library
The Library of Congress in Washington, USA, contains 28 million books and pamphlets, arranged on 940 km (584 miles) of shelves.

NEWSPAPER RECORDS

First newspaper
The Dutch *Corantos* (Currents of news) appeared in 1620.

Top-selling paper
Japanese newspaper *Yomissi Shimbun* has an average circulation of 8,700,000 every day.

Most daily papers
India holds the record, producing 2,300 daily newspapers. It is followed by the USA with 1,586 titles.

Keenest readers
In Sweden, 574 newspapers are sold for every 1,000 people, and 54 kg (119 lb) of wood-pulp paper is used to produce them.

RADIO AND TELEVISION

ALMOST EVERY HOME has a television or radio, for entertainment and for receiving information. Radio waves were first used to send messages in the late 1890s; broadcasting began in 1906. By the 1950s, television was widespread.

RADIO RECORDS

First radio message
In 1895, Marconi used radio waves to send messages. In 1901, he succeeded in sending a signal over the Atlantic.

First radio broadcast
In 1906, music and Bible readings by Reginald Fessenden of Canada were broadcast.

First commercial radio
In 1920, KDKA of Pittsburgh, USA went on the air with the results of the presidential elections.

First transistor radio
Introduced by Regency Electronics of the USA in 1954, tiny transistors replaced bulky valves. Radios became much smaller and more compact, and worked immediately instead of crackling while they warmed up.

First FM broadcast
The first VHF-FM stereo broadcasts were transmitted by KDKA-FM (see left) in 1960.

Longest running show
The show *Rambling with Gambling* was first broadcast in March 1925 on WOR-NY radio in New York, USA. It is still transmitted six days a week.

PEOPLE'S PHILCO RADIO SET, 1936

Longest running soap
The Archers, first broadcast by the BBC, UK, in January 1951, is still running today.

Largest audience
BBC radio's World Service has at least 120 million regular listeners all around the world.

Most radios
More than 2,000 radio sets are owned for every 1,000 people living in the USA today.

FIRST TRANSISTOR RADIO

TELEVISION RECORDS

First television
In 1926, engineer John Logie Baird, showed off his televisor, which broadcast a blurred face.

First TV broadcast
In 1929, the BBC broadcast Baird's pictures and in 1930, they were transmitted with sound added.

First TV camera
In 1932, Vladimir Zworykin invented an electronic TV camera.

First colour pictures
Colour pictures were transmitted in 1953 by the US company CBS.

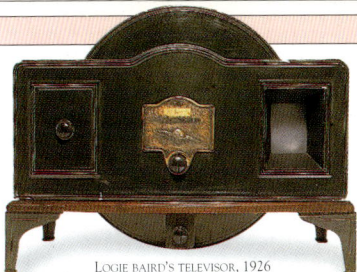

LOGIE BAIRD'S TELEVISOR, 1926

Longest-running programme
NBC's weekly *Meet the Press* was first broadcast in the USA in 1947.

Most dedicated viewers
On average, Americans watch 49.35 hours of television each week.

Largest audience
About 138.5 million people tuned in to the Super Bowl XXX on 28 January 1996.

Smallest TV
Seiko, Japan, launched the 3-cm (1⅛-in) TV-Wrist Watch in 1982.

VIDEO RECORDS

First video tape
Part of Sony's U-Matic system, the first video tapes appeared in 1970.

SONY U-MATIC
VIDEO CASSETTE, 1970

First video recorder
Phillips invented a home video recorder in 1972.

Fastest video on sale
The wedding of HRH Prince Andrew and Sarah Ferguson went on sale within 5 hours!

Best-selling video ever
Disney's *The Lion King* sold 20 million copies in its first six months.

FIRST SATELLITE
BROADCAST
Space satellites were launched in Canada in 1979 to beam TV and radio signals worldwide.

STAGE AND SCREEN

THE THEATRE we know today has its origins in ancient Greece, 2,500 years ago. Cinema only began to develop at the end of the 19th century, but it is now a multi-million pound industry worldwide.

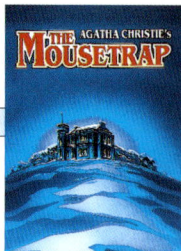

MOUSETRAP POSTER

THEATRE RECORDS

Oldest theatre
The first theatres were built in ancient Greece in the 5th century BC. Most could seat at least 18,000 spectators.

Smallest theatre
The Piccolo in Hamburg, Germany, is the smallest professional theatre, with seating for no more than 30 people.

Top theatre-goers
On average, each Cuban goes to the theatre 2.5 times a year.

Unluckiest play
In the theatre world, it is considered unlucky to say the name of Shakespeare's play, *Macbeth*. Instead, actors refer to it as "the Scottish play".

Longest running play
Agatha Christie's *The Mousetrap* opened in London in 1952. It has now been performed more than 20,000 times.

DANCE RECORDS

Longest conga
Some 119,986 people joined the Miami Super Conga in 1988 – the longest conga ever!

MIAMI SUPER CONGA

Oldest ballet
Ballo, an Italian dance with a storyline, was the earliest form of ballet, performed in the 1400s.

First ballerina en pointe
In 1832, Italian Marie Taglioni danced *en pointe* (on tiptoe).

Fastest tap dance
English dancer Stephen Gare performed 32 taps a minute in 1990.

First rock and roll
Teenagers of the 1950s enjoyed rock and roll, which first developed as a social dance.

CINEMA HISTORY RECORDS

First working camera
The first working film camera (kinetograph) and film viewer (kinetoscope) were developed by American, Thomas Edison and his British assistant, W.K.L. Dickson, in 1894.

First projection system
In Paris in 1895, French brothers, Auguste and Louis Lumière demonstrated the first system that could show films. They put a light behind the camera and ran the film through.

First talking film
The first "talkie" was *The Jazz Singer*, made in 1927. The soundtrack for the film was made as a separate recording.

THREE-STRIP TECHNICOLOR CAMERA

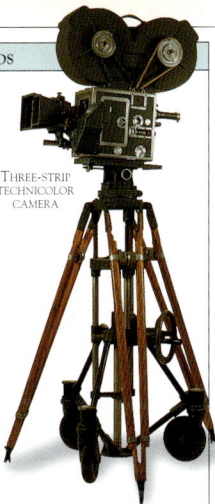

First colour camera
Technicolor cameras were invented in 1932. Films were coloured by hand before colour film was developed in 1937.

FILM RECORDS

Most films made
India's film industry produces more than 800 full-length feature films a year, twice as many as the USA.

Longest film made
The Cure for Insomnia (1987), directed by J.H. Timmis of the USA, lasted 85 hours!

First animated film
The cartoon *Humorous Phases of Funny Faces*, 1906, was composed of 3,000 drawings.

First Disney feature
The feature-length *Snow White and the Seven Dwarfs* was made in 1937.

REELS OF FILM

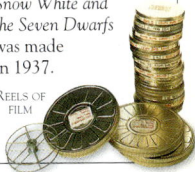

OSCAR RECORDS

First Oscars
The first Oscars (Academy Awards), were presented in the USA in 1929.

OSCAR

Most Oscars won
In 1959, the blockbuster *Ben Hur*, won a record 11 Oscars. *Gone with the Wind* (1939) and *West Side Story* (1961) each won ten Oscars.

First animated film nominated
In 1991, Disney's animated film *Beauty and the Beast* was nominated for the "best picture" Oscar.

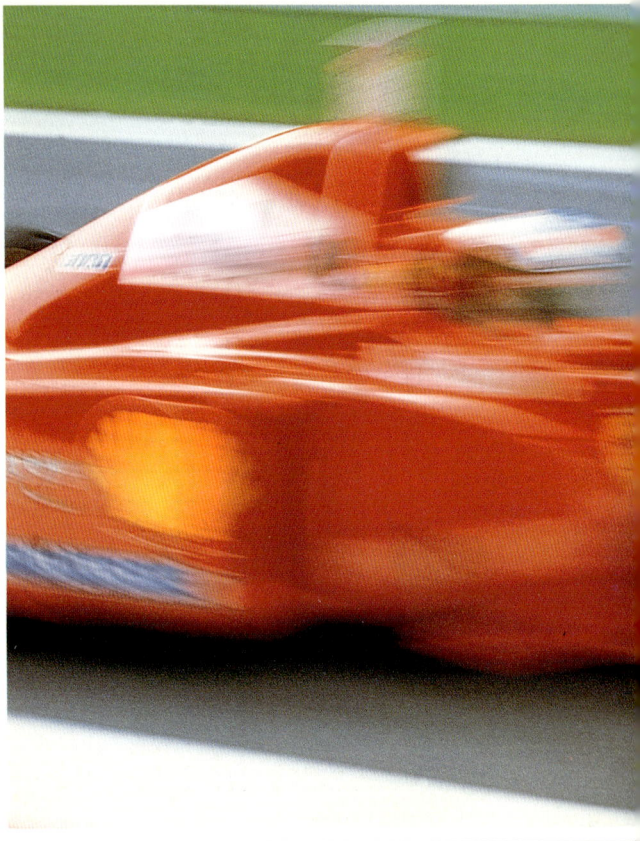

SPORT

Most used racing track: Monza circuit, Italy

BALL GAMES

SOME OF THE world's most popular sports are ball games. Soccer, rugby, American football, basketball, and volleyball all have huge followings of fans. An early form of football, the world's most played ball game, was invented in Italy in the 1400s.

HAND-PAINTED CLAY BALLS, C. 2,000 BC

FIRST BALLS
These early clay balls suggest that ball games were played in ancient Egypt 4,000 years ago.

SOCCER RECORDS

First football boots
Early steel or chrome toe-capped football boots of the 1880s protected the feet but were heavy to wear.

Highest scoring game
In 1935, *Tranmere Rovers* and *Oldham Athletic*, UK, scored 17 goals in one game.

WORLD CUP

EARLY 20TH-CENTURY BOOT

Steel toe-caps protected the player's feet

Top World Cup team
Brazil has won the World Cup no fewer than four times.

Largest crowd
In 1950, 199,854 fans watched Brazil play Uruguay in a World Cup match in Rio de Janeiro, Brazil.

Most goals scored in a World Cup game
In the 1994 World Cup, Oleg Salenko of Russia scored five goals against Cameroon.

RUGBY RECORDS

First game of rugby
Rugby was first played at Rugby School, UK in 1823.

RUGBY BALL, 1851

First rugby ball
The first balls used in the game of rugby were much rounder in shape than those used today.

Longest goal kick
In 1932, a rugby ball was kicked a distance of 82 m (270 ft).

AMERICAN FOOTBALL RECORDS

First game played
American football was first played in 1874. The game was a mixture of rugby and soccer.

Largest shoulder pads
The biggest shoulder pads are usually worn by offensive and defensive linesmen.

SHOULDER AND CHEST PAD

BIKE

BIKE

AIR-LITE

BLUE LASER

Pads can weigh up to 2.5 kg (5½ lb)

Best college team
Alabama, USA, has the best record, with the *University of Southern California*, USA, coming close behind.

Most Super Bowl wins
Both the *San Francisco 49ers* and the *Dallas Cowboys* have won the USA's Super Bowl a record five times.

Super Bowl win
In the USA's 1990 Super Bowl, the *San Francisco 49ers* beat the *Denver Broncos* by a record 45 points!

BASKETBALL RECORDS

First basketball game
American Dr J. Naismith invented basketball in 1891. He hung the baskets from his balcony.

Most world wins
The former USSR's women's team won no less than six World Championships.

Highest score
At the Asian Games in 1982, Iraq beat Yemen by 251–3 – the highest ever international score.

Most famous team
The *Harlem Globetrotters* of the USA are world famous.

Tallest player
Suleiman Nashnush (1943–1991) of Libya was 2.45 m (8 ft ¼ in) tall.

HARLEM GLOBETROTTER

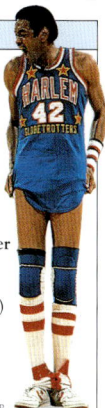

VOLLEYBALL RECORDS

First volleyball game
American sports' instructor William Morgan invented volleyball in 1895.

First beach volleyball
Beach volleyball was first played in the USA in the 1940s. It made its Olympic debut in 1996.

Most Olympic golds
The USSR's men's team won Olympic gold three times; the women's team four.

STICK AND RACKET GAMES

Knocking off the bails means you're out!

TEAM GAMES such as hockey, cricket, and baseball are among the most popular stick games, played with a small ball. Racket games involve fewer players.

FIRST THIRD STUMP!
In cricket, a third stump was introduced to stop the ball passing between the two outer stumps.

CRICKET RECORDS

First cricket bats
The first cricket bats had curved blades and appeared in the 1700s.

First Test Match
The first cricket Test Match was played in Melbourne in 1877 between England and Australia.

Most runs of all time
Between 1978 and 1992, Allan Border of Australia made 11,174 test match runs.

Top wicket taker
India's Kapil Dev took a record 434 test wickets in his 24-year career.

Most centuries
Sunil Gavaskar of India, has scored 34 centuries.

"Cricket" comes from "cric", meaning shepherd's crook, which early bats resembled.

CRICKET BAT, 18TH CENTURY

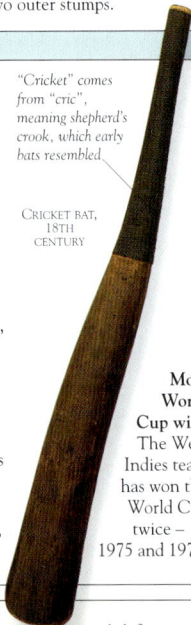

HOCKEY RECORDS

First hockey game
Hockey, as we know the game today, was invented as recently as the late 1880s.

Most Olympic golds
India has won Olympic gold eight times. The last time was in 1980.

Most World Cup wins
The Netherlands team won the women's world cup five times. Pakistan has won the men's four times.

Most World Cup wins
The West Indies team has won the World Cup twice – in 1975 and 1979.

GOALKEEPER'S HELMET

BASEBALL RECORDS

First baseball game
Baseball was first played in the USA in the mid-1800s.

Oldest stadia
Both the USA's Tiger Stadium and Fenway Park were built in 1912.

Most runs scored
Ty Cobb of the USA scored 2,245 runs during his career.

Most World Series wins
The *New York Yankees* have won this 23 times!

FIELDING GLOVE

TENNIS RECORDS

LAWN TENNIS RACKET, 1880

Early tennis rackets were loosely strung

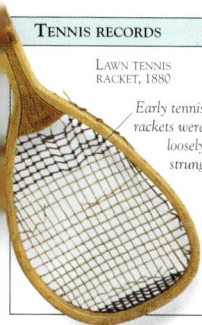

First tennis match
Tennis was first played in France by members of the clergy and royalty.

First strung rackets
Strung rackets were in use by the 15th century.

Oldest championship
The Wimbledon tennis championship, UK, was first held in 1877.

Most Grand Slam wins
Australia's Margaret Court won 26 titles.

Youngest champion
In 1985, 17-year-old Boris Becker won at Wimbledon.

Most singles titles
Martina Navratilova, USA won nine Wimbledon titles.

MORE RACKET RECORDS

First racketball championship
The USA held the first racketball World Championship in 1982.

Greatest squash champion
Pakistan's Jahangir Khan has won the World Championship six times!

Top badminton champions
The Indonesian men's team has won the World Championship nine times.

RECORD GOLFER
American golfer, Tiger Woods (b. 1975), is the youngest winner of the US Amateur Championships and the first African-American to play on the PGA (Professional Golf Association) tour.

TIGER WOODS

WATER SPORTS

THOUSANDS OF people take part in sailing, rowing, surfing, and water-skiing. Swimming did not become popular until the 1800s as it was thought unhygienic. Now, it is one of the most practised forms of exercise.

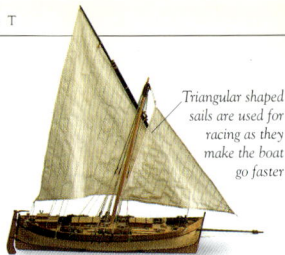

Triangular shaped sails are used for racing as they make the boat go faster

FIRST TRIANGULAR SAILS
Triangular lateen sails replaced square sails around 200 BC. Boats could then sail and race faster against the wind.

BOATING AND YACHTING RECORDS

First round-the-world race
The Whitbread Round-the-World race, 60,000 km (38,000 miles) long, was first held in 1973.

Most boats racing
A record 2,072 boats began Denmark's 1984 Round Zeeland race.

Longest powerboat race
The 1972 powerboat race between the River Thames, UK, and Monte Carlo, Monaco, covered 4,742 km (2,947 miles).

Longest sailing race
The record for the 41,652-km (25,883-mile) Vendée Globe Challenge is 109.5 days.

Fastest under sail
In 1993, *Yellow Pages Endeavour* reached 86.21 km/h (53.57 mph) off Australia.

Most America's Cups
The USA has won the America's Cup 27 out of 29 times. Its two defeats were at the hands of Australia, and then New Zealand.

Fastest speed on water
In 1978, Ken Warby broke the water speed record in *Spirit of Australia*, reaching a speed of 514 km/h (320 mph). The record still stands today.

SPIRIT OF AUSTRALIA

Hydroplane has a jet engine

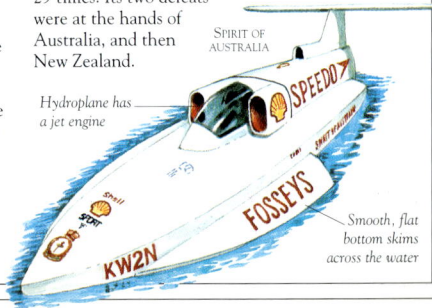

SPEEDO

FOSSEYS

KW2N

Smooth, flat bottom skims across the water

SURFING RECORDS

First surfing contest
World Championships
for professional surfers
were first held in 1970.

Most surfing titles
Mark Richards of
Australia holds five
World surfing titles.

**First Olympic
windsurfing event**
Developed in 1958,
windsurfing became an
Olympic event in 1984.

Fastest windsurfer
Thierry Bielak, France,
surfed at a record-
breaking 83 km/h
(52 mph) in 1991.

ROWING AND CANOEING RECORDS

First rowing race
Rowing races were held
in England in the early
1700s. Today, rowing is
an Olympic sport.

Most gold medals
Giuseppe and Carmine
Abbagnale, Italy, and
Steven Redgrave, UK,
have each won nine
rowing golds at Olympic
and World events.

Fastest kayak
At the 1995 World
Championships, the
Hungarian four-man
kayak team won with
an average speed of
23 km/h (14 mph).

Longest canoe race
In 1967, a race starting
in Alberta, Canada, ran
for 5,283 km (3,283
miles) to Montreal.

FASTEST ON WATER SKIS
The record speed for
water skiing is an
incredible 230 km/h
(143 mph). A skier
must travel at 30 km/h
(19 mph) to keep upright.

SWIMMING AND DIVING RECORDS

Fastest stroke
Front crawl is the fastest
swimming stroke, and is
most commonly used in
freestyle races.

Slowest stroke
Breaststroke is the
slowest, as the swimmer's
arms and legs remain
underwater throughout.

BREASTSTROKE SWIMMER

First highboard dive
The 1904 Olympics
included highboard
diving, with the board
10 m (33 ft) above water.

First springboard dive
Diving off a springy 3-m
(10-ft) board became an
Olympic sport in 1908.

Legs kick   Arms push forward
outwards   and circle
                   round

Most gold medals
Mark Spitz of the
USA won seven gold
medals at the Olympic
Games in 1972.

**First synchronized
swimming event**
Synchronized swimming
events were first held
at the Olympic Games
in Los Angeles in 1984.
Synchronized swimmers
are all women.

WINTER SPORTS

FOR EXCITEMENT, speed, and skill, winter sports are hard to beat. Even if you do not take part in them, you can share the thrills of skating, skiing, ice hockey, and sledging by watching the Winter Olympic Games, held every four years.

Boots were tied to animal bones

FIRST ICE SKATES
The earliest iron skate known comes from Scandinavia, AD 200. Bones were used as blades.

ICE HOCKEY RECORDS

First Olympic ice hockey
Making its debut at the 1920 Summer games, ice hockey is now part of the Winter Games.

Fastest game in the world
In ice hockey, players skate at speeds of 50 km/h (31 mph) and hit the puck at up to 190 km/h (118 mph)!

ICE HOCKEY EQUIPMENT

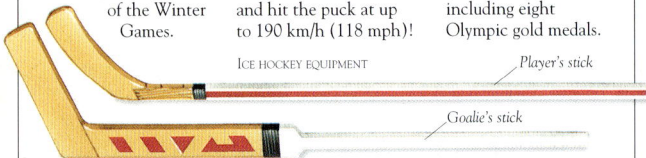

Most world titles
The USSR/Unified Team won 22 world ice hockey titles between 1954 and 1990, including eight Olympic gold medals.

Player's stick

Goalie's stick

ICE SKATING RECORDS

First ice skating
Skating on frozen canals first became popular in the Netherlands during the 1200s. Skating is still enjoyed today.

Most pairs titles won
British ice dancers Jayne Torvill and Christopher Dean won seven titles between 1978 and 1983, and in 1994.

Speediest skater
In 1989, dutch speed skater, Dries van Wijhe, skated 200 km (124 miles) in five hours and forty minutes.

SLED RECORDS

Rarest event
The toboggan event has only been held in 1928 and 1948 at St Moritz's Winter Games.

Fastest tobogganer
In 1992, Bertschinger of Switzerland went down the Cresta Run at an average speed of 86 km/h (54 mph).

Top four-man team
Switzerland has won the world four-man bob title a record 20 times.

Skin-tight suit and helmet

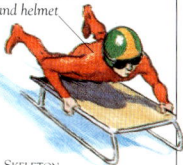

SKELETON
TOBOGGANING

SKIING RECORDS

First cross-country
The first cross-country ski race was held in Norway in 1843.

First downhill racing
Downhill racing dates back to 1911. It is the fastest type of racing with competitors reaching speeds of 140 km/h (87 mph).

First slalom racing
Slalom racing, in which the skiier has to negotiate a series of gates, was first held in 1922.

First biathlon
A combination of cross-country skiing and rifle shooting, the biathlon event made its Olympic debut in 1960 for men and 1992 for women.

MODERN SKIS

Alpine skis are heavier and wider than Nordic skis

Modern skis must have sharp, smooth edges

Longest ski jump
In March 1996, Austrian Andreas Goldberger jumped 204 m (670 ft).

Speed record
The fastest person on skis is American Jeffrey Hamilton, at 241 km/h (150 mph).

WINTER OLYMPIC RECORDS

First Winter Olympics
First held in 1924 at Chamonix, the Winter Olympics include five sports: figure skating, ice hockey, Nordic skiing, bobsleigh, and speed skating.

Most competitors
A record number of 1,737 participants from no fewer than 67 different countries competed in the 1994 Winter Games at Lillehammer, Norway.

Double winner
Edward Eagan (USA) became the only person to win gold at Summer and Winter Olympics. He was champion of boxing and the four-man bob in 1932.

HORSE RACING

THOROUGHBRED racehorses were first bred in Europe in the late 1600s, but racing dates back centuries. Today, the sport comprises flat racing and jump racing.

WORLD'S OLDEST HORSE RACE
Run since medieval times, the Palio takes place every summer in Siena, Italy.

HORSE RIDING AND RACING RECORDS

First saddle
Cushioned saddles were invented in China, between AD 25 and 220. They made horse riding easier and more comfortable.

First Olympic horse events
The three equestrian events – dressage, cross country and show jumping – have been part of the Olympic Games since 1912.

First horse-driving
Three-day international horse-driving trials began in 1970.

Top jockey
American jockey, Willie Shoemaker, rode a record 8,833 winners in his 42-year career.

Fastest racehorse
Big Racket achieved a top speed of 69.62 km/h (43.26 mph) over a distance of 402 m (¼ mile) during a race in Mexico City in 1945.

All racehorses must be Thoroughbreds

THOROUGHBRED HORSE AND JOCKEY

Silk shirt and hat shows owner's racing colours

MOST FAMOUS RACE
The *Grand National* is run over 6.4 km (4 miles) at Aintree racecourse, UK The famous horse *Red Rum* has won this gruelling steeplechase three times – in 1973, 1974, and 1977.

Helmets are covered in coloured silk

JOCKEY'S HELMET

Lead weights are used to handicap the fastest horses

MOTOR RACING

OF ALL THE different types of motor racing, high-speed Formula One is amongst the most watched, with 17 races worldwide. Rallying and Indycar racing also have many fans.

BEST-KNOWN SPORTS CAR RACE
First run in 1923, the Le Mans 24-hours race is held every year at Le Mans, near Paris, France.

RALLY AND INDY CAR RACING

Most famous rally
The Monte Carlo rally was first held in 1911.

Longest rally ever
The London–Sydney Rally (1977) was 31,107 km (19,329 miles) long.

Longest annual rally
Kenya's annually held Safari Rally covers 6,000 km (3,728 miles).

Best known Indy track
Indianapolis circuit is 4 km (2 ½ miles) long.

Top Indycar driver
Al Unser (USA) won the Indy 500 a record-equalling four times.

Fastest Indycar speed
An Indycar travelled at 385 km/h (239 mph).

FORMULA ONE RECORDS

Youngest champion
Brazilian Emerson Fittipaldi became the world champion in 1972 aged 25 years, 9 months.

Most World titles won
Juan Manuel Fangio, of Argentina, won five world titles between 1911 and 1995.

Most Grand Prix wins
Prost (France) won 51 races from 1981–1993.

Top manufacturer
Ferrari of Italy won the manufacturers' World Championship a record eight times between 1961 and 1983.

FERRARI RACING CAR

Closest finish
In the 1986 Spanish Grand Prix, Brazil's Ayrton Senna beat the UK's Nigel Mansell by just 0.014 seconds.

Sponsor's logo

OLYMPIC GAMES

OLYMPIA, GREECE, was host to the earliest ever games in 776 BC. They were then held every four years, in honour of the god, Zeus. The first modern Olympic Games – the brainchild of Frenchman, Baron Pierre de Coubertin – were held in Athens, Greece, in 1896.

FIRST MARATHON
In 490 BC, a Greek raced 39 km (24 miles) with news of the Battle of Marathon.

FIRST THROWING EVENT
The discus was one of the first throwing events. Athletes symbolized the peak of fitness and many statues were made of them.

ANCIENT OLYMPIC RECORDS

First Olympic prize
A wreath of sacred olive leaves was the first prize for winners of the ancient Olympic Games. There were no gold medals.

OLIVE WREATH

First Olympic event
A sprint over a distance of 185 m (606 ft), or one length of the running track, made up the first Olympic event.

First jumps
The long jump was one of the first Olympic events. Greeks were used to leaping over streams and ditches in rugged countryside so it came naturally!

First Olympic guide
Roman Pausanias wrote an Olympic programme when he visited Olympia in AD 170.

Last ancient Olympics
In AD 393, Christian Emperor Theodosius abolished the Games as the obsession with the physical was thought to be morally wrong.

MODERN OLYMPIC RECORDS

First to discover Olympia
Having lain forgotten for 1,000 years, Olympia was rediscovered in 1766 by Englishman Richard Chandler.

First modern Olympics
Athens, Greece, played host to the first modern Olympics in 1896.

First Olympic Village
The 1932 Los Angeles games had a purpose-built Olympic Village.

First Olympic flame
Held by relay runners, the Olympic flame first blazed at the 1928 Amsterdam Games.

OLYMPIC SYMBOL

Rings represent the countries taking part in the games

First Olympic flag
First flown at Antwerp, Belgium, in 1920, the official Olympic flag has five rings that represent the world.

First footage of games
The first newsreel footage of the Olympics dates from 1912. The first feature-length film dates from 1924.

First televised games
The 1936 Berlin Olympic Games were the first to be televised. Today, millions of people watch the Olympics on TV.

Most competitors
A total of 10,768 athletes from 197 nations competed in the 1996 Atlanta Games.

PARALYMPIC RECORDS

First Paralympics
Olympics for disabled athletes were first held in Rome, in 1960.

Fastest swimmers
Blind Paralympic swimmers have come within one-hundredth of a second of the qualifying time for the US Olympic team.

Top female athlete
Wheelchair-bound Louise Sauvage (Aus), holds the women's 400 m, 800 m, 1,500 m and 5,000 m records.

Record crowds
The 1992 Paralympics held in Barcelona, Spain, drew a crowd of 1.5 million spectators.

LOUISE SAUVAGE, SPRINT CHAMPION

OLYMPIC WORLD RECORDS

FOR TODAY'S TOP athletes, winning an Olympic gold medal is a dream come true, the pinnacle of their athletic careers. For others, simply taking part is a thrill in itself.

1996
ATLANTA OLYMPICS,
GOLD MEDAL

TRACK AND ROAD EVENT RECORDS				
EVENT	MALE	TIME	FEMALE	TIME
100-m sprint	D. Bailey	9.84 s	F. Griffith-Joyner	10.62 s
200-m sprint	M. Johnson	19.32 s	F. Griffith-Joyner	21.34 s
400-m sprint	M. Johnson	43.49 s	M.J. Perec	48.25 s
800-m middle	V. Rodal	1 m 42.58 s	N. Olizarenko	1 m 53.43 s
1,500-m middle	S. Coe	3 m 32.53 s	P. Ivan	3 m 53.96 s
5,000-m long	S. Aouita	13 m 5.59 s	W. Junxia	14 m 59.88 s
10,000-m long	H. Gebrselassie	27 m 7.34 s	F. Riberio	31 m 1.03 s
4 x 100-m relay	USA team	37.40 s	GDR team	41.60 s
4 x 400-m relay	USA team	2 m 55.74 s	URS team	3 m 15.17 s
100-m hurdles	No men's event		Y. Donkova	12.38 s
110-m hurdles	A. Johnson	12.95 s	No women's event	
400-m hurdles	K. Young	46.78 s	D. Hemmings	52.82 s
3,000-m steeple	J. Kariuki	8 m 5.51 s	No women's event	
Marathon	C. Lopes	2 h 9 m 21 s	J. Benoit	2 h 24 m 52 s
10-km walk	No men's event		Y. Nikolayera	41 m 49 s
20-km walk	J. Pribilinec	1 h 19 m 57 s	No women's event	
50-km walk	V. Ivanenko	3 h 38 m 29 s	No women's event	

ATHLETE RECORDS

First black African gold medallist
In 1960, Abebe Bikila ran the marathon barefoot and became the first black African to win gold.

First brothers to win Olympic medal
Laurie and Reggie Doherty won the men's tennis doubles at the 1900 Olympics held in Paris, France.

First perfect ten
At the 1976 Montreal Games, Romanian gymnast Nadia Comaneci scored the first ever perfect ten.

Oldest female Olympic gold medallist
Lia Manoliu of Romania was 36 years old when she won the discus at the 1968 Olympics in Mexico.

Greatest record-breaker
In the 1968 Mexico Olympics, American Bob Beamon increased the long jump record by 55 cm (21¼ in).

BRAVEST OLYMPIC WINNER
Jesse Owens, USA, defied the Nazi idea of white supremacy at the 1936 Berlin Olympics and won four gold medals.

Owens excelled at sprinting

JESSE OWENS

OLYMPIC JUMPING EVENTS

EVENT		ATHLETE	DISTANCE
High jump	(m)	C. Austin	2.39 m
	(f)	S. Kostadinova	2.05 m
Long jump	(m)	B. Beamon	8.90 m
	(f)	J. Joyner-Kersee	7.40 m
Triple jump	(m)	K. Harrison	18.09 m
	(f)	I. Kravets	15.33 m
Pole vault	(m)	J. Galfione	5.92 m

OLYMPIC THROWING RECORDS

EVENT		WEIGHT	ATHLETE	DISTANCE
Javelin	(m)	0.8 kg	J. Zelezny	89.66 m
	(f)	0.6 kg	P. Felke	74.68 m
Discus	(m)	2 kg	L. Riedel	69.40 m
	(f)	1 kg	M. Hellmann	83.22 m
Shot put	(m)	7.26 kg	U. Timmermann	22.47 m
	(f)	4 kg	I. Slupianek	22.41 m
Hammer	(m)	7.26 kg	S. Litvinov	84.80 m

FIELD EQUIPMENT

Index

Acknowledgements

PAGEOne and DK would like to thank:
Hilary Bird for the index, Roby Braun for
model making, Chris Clark for DTP assistance,
Euro Models, Hendon Way Motors, Nick
Hughes and Tim Smith, Pegasus Stables,
Newmarket, Pitt Rivers Museum, Motorcycle
Heritage Museum, Westerville, Ohio, Museum
of London, Museum of the Moving Image,
National Maritime Museum, National Railway
Museum, York, St Bride Printing Library,
The University Museum of Archaeology
and Anthropology, Cambridge, and
University Museum of Zoology, Cambridge.

Cover: photograph reproduced by courtesy
of TI Group PLC, photography by Tony
Short Associates, art direction by Cairnes.

Special photographers:
G. Brightling, A. Crawford, G. Dann, P. Dowell,
L. Fordes, L. Gardiner, P. Gatward, S. Gorton,
F. Greenaway, P. Hayman, J. Heseltine,
C. Howson, C. Keates, D. King, R. Moller,
D. Rudkin, C. Streeter, M. Ward, J. Young.

Illustrators:
E. Anderson, E. Antoniou, R. Barnett,
R. Bonson, P. Bull, L. Corbella, M. Courtney,
P. Dennis, B.Donohoe, W. Donahoe, E. Fleury,
G. Fornari, R. Grinaway, N. Hewetson, R. Lewis,
K. Lilly, R. Lindsay, S. Milne, P. Morter,
A. Pang, D. Pyne, S. Quigley, R. Shackell,
C. Spong, J. Temperton, R. Ward, J. Woodcock.

Picture credits:
t=top b=bottom c=centre l=left r=right
Action plus/Glyn Kirk 121 b; AKG London
120 bl; Allsport 111 b/Michael Cooper 108-
109/Stephen Dunn 122; Archive photos/Kean
59 b; Bridgeman Art Library/Louvre, Paris 100
bc/Vatican Museums & Art; Galleries,
Rome 94-95; British Dental Association 73 b;
British Museum 110 tr; Capitoline Museum,
Rome 58; Bruce Coleman Ltd/Norman
Tomalin 26-27; Colorific/Jenny Quiggin 79;
Diners Club 64 c; European Space Agency
91 b; Mary Evans Picture Library 59 t, 84 cr,
103 tr; Getty Images/Donovan Reese 21 tr;
Glasgow Museums 105 t; Robert Harding
Picture Library 54-55/Philip Craven 92 r;
Hutchison Library/Bernard Regent 68-69/
David Clilverd 77 b; Leica camera Ltd 101b;
London Transport Museum 85 t; The
Mousetrap Foundation 106 t; N.A.S.A. 91 cl,
91 tr; National Motor Museum, Beaulieu 82 t;
National Postal Museum 92 c; National Rail
Museum 80 b, 81 cl; Stephen Oliver 62 br;
Robert Opie Collection 92 bl; Panos Pictures/
Alain le Garsmeur 20 tr; Vassili Papastavrou
50 tr; Planet Earth Library/Gary Bell 17 br;
Rex Features 123 t/Butler/Bauer 24 br/DiPaola
113 b/Sipa Press 65; Science and Society
Picture Library 71 t; Science Museum, London
61 tr, 63 t, 67 br, 71 bl, 80 tl, 81 b, 98 cl, 102 tr,
104 b; Science Photo Library/Peter Menzell
24 cl; Smithsonian Institute 72 t, 72 b, 73 t,
73 c, 86 c, 93 tl; Sony U.K. Ltd 99 cl, 105 bl;
South American Pictures/Tony Morrison 10-11;
Frank Spooner Pictures/Kaku Kurita/ Gamma
77 tr; St Bride Printing Library 102 br; Straker
Welds 104 t; Telstar Canada 105 br; University
Museum of Zoology, Cambridge 51 tr; York
Archaeology Trust/Simon I Hill 116 t

Every effort has been made to trace the
copyright holders and we apologise in
advance for any unintentional omissions.
We would be pleased to insert the
appropriate acknowledgement in any
subsequent edition of this publication.